Lynne Freeman, Ph. D.

W9-BRD-791

PANIC FREE

Eliminate Anxiety/Panic Attacks Without Drugs and Take Control of Your Life

Foreword by
Arnold Fox M.D.

Library of Congress Catalog card number
Freeman, Lynne, 1955-
    Panic Free: eliminate anxiety/panic attacks without drugs and take control of your life/by Lynne Freeman
    Includes bibliography references and index.
    ISBN 0-9668456-0-8 (pbk.)
    98-93811

Published by Arden Books
Sherman Oaks, CA

Printed in United States of America

Revised Edition

In loving memory of my father,
Lee Edwin Freeman,
whose vision, generosity and sensitivity
have enabled me to attain my dreams

ACKNOWLEDGMENTS

With deep gratitude to my mother, Dvora Freeman, for her love, patience and encouragement.

Special thanks to Terry Sherf, without whom this book might not have been published. And to Deanne Sorola for her valuable editing contributions.

Thanks to Leah Fein, M.A. for her personal and professional support. To Jenna Evans, for marching with me into hell and back. To Susan Holt for opening closed doors and illuminating the darkness.

I wish to thank my agents Rosalie Heacock and her late husband, Jim.

And last but certainly not least to Stan Freeman for giving me the sun, the moon and the stars.

Bravo Dr. Freeman!

With due respect to the doctors whose book endorsements accompany this one, medical science has somehow managed to wallow in the dark ages where the functional diagnosis and treatment of Anxiety Disorders is concerned. I suffered the agonies of hell through a wide range of Fear and Panic attacks over a period of twenty-two years, only to be bandied from therapist to therapist poking and probing into my forgotten past in some antiquated Freudian witch-hunt designed to relive some magic event or impression that would instantly make me well. Naturally, there was none. Dr. Freeman, more advisedly, deals with the self-induced ravishes of Anxiety in the much more practical and treatable arena of the NOW and TODAY and, of course, finds her rightful success.

Marty Ingels
Author/Comedian

TABLE OF CONTENTS

PREFACE

It was nearly twenty years ago when I experienced my first panic attack. The Diagnostic and Statistical Manual of Psychiatric Disorders labeled my symptoms "anxiety neurosis." This neurosis was believed to be caused by unconscious desires that were subjugated by an overly active super ego. My psychotherapist maintained that my symptoms were a manifestation of birth trauma which, for some inexplicable reason, were being triggered and causing me to feel anxious. When he could not help me, I was left on my own with a dearth of information on the subject and no resources for support.

Fortunately, a great deal has changed since then. The National Institute of Mental Health has labeled anxiety the nation's number one mental health problem! There has been an explosion of research into the biological etiology of anxiety disorders. The 1990's have been declared and exemplified as the "Age of Anxiety" as greater numbers of individuals acknowledge and recognize the existence of anxiety in their lives.

Additionally, with the development of more sophisticated medications to manage anxiety, a revolution of sorts has been gaining momentum. Scores of individuals are prescribed antidepressant medication every day as these medications are now considered the first line of defense to combat symptoms of anxiety. They are, indeed, very impressive. But what if you are one of the thirty percent of the population who does not improve with medication or you found that the effectiveness wore off over time? Perhaps you are one of the fifty percent of mental health patients that has a medical problem which has been overlooked by your physician. Instead of proper diagnosis and treatment of your medical symptoms, you may have been prescribed tranquilizers and/or antidepressants prematurely. Some of these may even be contraindicated for your particular medical condition. Perhaps you are healthy and the drugs you are taking manage your anxiety quite well, but you were informed by your doctor that you may need to take them indefinitely. You feel uncomfortable with this, or, you may simply be frustrated by having to choose between accepting the side effects of some medications or being anxious. Despite what you may have read, heard, or been told by a physician or psychiatrist, overcoming anxiety is not an either/or proposition. You do not have to take medication to get better. This book was written to offer you choices. It does not attempt to persuade or dissuade you from taking drugs. Rather, it provides proven methods which are effective with or without the use of medication.

You will learn about the different medical conditions that mimic anxiety symptoms, how to assess your own anxiety, the benefits of both medication and alternative medicine, and specific tools and techniques that you can use to ameliorate your symptoms. Each person is different and no particular solution is appropriate for everyone. It is my intent to provide you with as much information as possible to assist you in making well-informed decisions about your own treatment.

ANXIETY IS A TREATABLE DISEASE. Your commitment to recovery will give you the patience, determination, and self-caring to practice the techniques that will meet your goal of successful living!

> Dr. Lynne Freeman, Director
> OPEN DOORS INSTITUTE
> Sherman Oaks, California

FOREWORD

Reading Dr. Lynne Freeman's book *Panic Free: Eliminate Anxiety /Panic Attacks and Take Control of Your Life Without Drugs* filled me with excitement. Finally, a book on anxiety that sets forth the various anxiety and panic states, and more importantly, what to do for the individual to recognize and ameliorate the symptoms—many of which can appear to be life threatening to the patient.

Where was this book when I was a young resident in internal medicine at the Los Angeles County Hospital seeing patients with anxiety? My colleagues and I were often misled into therapeutic misadventures sometimes perilous to the patients.

Anxiety and panic disorders are an important cause of concern because patients will make frequent visits to their physicians and to emergency departments seeking immediate relief for their symptoms. They are then subjected to unnecessary and, at times, dangerous tests which are most often not productive, costly of time and finances, and frustrating to both physician and patient.

Over the years I can count many sleepless nights due to calls from Emergency Departments regarding patients with acute anxiety episodes seeking help for palpitations, shortness of breath and a collection of puzzling symptoms expertly quantified by Dr. Lynne Freeman. Every week I have seen one or more patients whose lives have been topsy-turvy because of the symptoms of their anxiety.

Dr. Lynne Freeman, with precise accuracy, weds style and substance. This book is so good that not only do I recommend it to those suffering from an anxiety disorder or those who know someone with such a problem but, more importantly, those who have unexplained and not substantially diagnosed medical symptoms.

Finally, I highly recommend this book to my medical colleagues. It provides exciting new innovations in the assessment and treatment of all types of anxiety disorders.

Arnold Fox, M.D.
Bestselling Author

INTRODUCTION

I was sitting in a college classroom when suddenly everything around me began to look strange and distorted. My heart started to pound. I felt as though something terrible was about to happen—something I couldn't define. My whole body began to shake, and I had an overwhelming urge to bolt for the door.

After a moment, I rose, left the classroom, then hurried down the hall and out to the parking lot. Once in my car, I leaned back and clicked on the ignition. My fingers were trembling. Though I lived only three blocks from campus, the drive home seemed to take forever. As I pulled to a stop at a red light, I noticed that the pavement in front of me appeared to be moving in waves. That was the longest red light I had ever waited for.

Upon reaching home, I began to feel a bit calmer. Still, I was confused and badly shaken by what happened. Someone must have put some sort of drug into the food I had eaten that morning, I decided. If I could just hold on until the effects wore off, I told myself, I would be okay. But the next day, it happened again. Since I was seeing a psychotherapist at the time, I quickly phoned his office.

He was very supportive. He explained that I had experienced an "anxiety attack"—and probably didn't ingest a hallucinogen, as I had thought. Still, I found it hard to believe that this bizarre and terrifying incident was of my own making.

With my therapist's help, I soon learned not to fear the attacks. Yet I remained uneasy, wondering if they would strike at any time. As a result, driving the car for any distance became frightening. Before long, I felt forced to limit both my driving and my life in general. As long as I stayed within the narrow parameters I had set, I was all right.

Eventually, the panic attacks subsided, and I felt fairly confident about traveling longer distances. But several years later, after a bout with illness, I suddenly experienced an anxiety attack on the way to my therapist's office. As before, he tried to calm me, but this time it didn't work. Though I increased my therapy sessions to several times a week, the anxieties worsened. Finally, my therapist told me he was not equipped to help me overcome my problem. He could not even provide me with a referral. I felt lost and totally helpless.

The anxieties soon limited me to traveling within a one-mile radius of my home. Trips that required driving further than this were avoided, since they were emotionally and physically draining. In time, I became completely agoraphobic, shut-in, afraid to go outside. I felt anxious even in my own home.

Ironically, I was pursuing a bachelor's degree in clinical psychology at the time. I was also in the second year of a relationship. Neither involvement seemed to help. Each passing day left me feeling more and more depressed. I grew extremely weak, and my health began to deteriorate. I lost twenty pounds from chronic diarrhea. I had also lost all interest in sexual relations and was constantly apologizing to my partner. I stopped seeing most of my friends because it meant having to drive somewhere to meet or to visit them.

On some days I was less anxious than on others. Only later did I learn that these peaks and valleys are typical of panic disorder. On those calmer days, I managed to attend the intern training meetings that were part of my bachelor's degree program. Then, on the final meeting day, my supervisors asked if I would like a part-time counseling job at the mental health clinic where I had been training. Since I had planned to fulfill my required counseling hours as a volunteer crisis counselor, being paid for my services would be a plus. I accepted—even though I knew the agency where I would be working was a half hour drive from home. But my determination to make that drive started to crumble as feelings of anxiety began to overwhelm me again.

This setback was a turning point for me. I decided that I had to overcome my fears once and for all. But how? The therapy sessions hadn't helped. Then, one night, my mother, a psychotherapist, visited me at home. She encouraged me to express what I was feeling. As we talked, I closed my eyes. I began to picture my anxiety as a huge monster that was bent on destroying my life. As the image grew clearer, I suddenly started to scream and to curse at it. I leaped up and, in a burst of rage, threw pillows around the room. At that moment, I realized the monster grew bigger and more powerful every time I gave in to it. Whenever I avoided a situation that might trigger anxieties I was letting the monster win. I had to show this monster that it no longer controlled me!

After that, I decided to "laugh" at the monster every time I sensed it was closing in on me—every time a pang of fear made me uneasy about doing something or going somewhere. In the days that followed, the more the "monster" tried to overpower me, the more strongly I resisted giving in to the anxieties it provoked. "You can't stop me," I told it, using anger to propel me forward. This time, I'm going to win—and I can!" Slowly, my anxieties started to subside as I continued to challenge my fears. And my life began to improve tremendously.

Looking back, I realize now that my improvement was due to a combination of factors. Psychotherapy was not among them, however. My therapist had dismissed me. And when I sought help from other professionals in the field, none of them seemed to know how to treat panic disorder. I had to find my own answers. Seeing the "monster" was the first of several innovative techniques that to the amazement of these therapists—soon enabled my recovery. I would like to share these and other promising approaches in the hope that you will explore them and go on to amaze someone—beginning with you!

Chapter 1

AGORAPHOBIA AND PANIC DISORDER

ALL ANXIETIES ARE NOT THE SAME

Because you are reading this book, chances are you have been experiencing what may have seemed like panic attacks. But how can you know for *sure*? What triggers these terrifying feelings and what is the right treatment to help relieve them? Keep in mind: anxieties are not all the same.

The first step is to determine whether you have actually been having panic attacks. This means obtaining an accurate diagnosis of your symptoms, preferably from a qualified psychotherapist. You may even be able to do this on your own, once you know the criteria doctors use to identify the various anxiety disorders.

These guidelines are spelled out at the end of this chapter. You may now want to take a peek at them to familiarize yourself with the various kinds of anxiety and where your symptoms may fall in the anxiety spectrum.

The reader will notice that the terms "client" and "patient" are used interchangeably, as are the use of personal pronouns, he, she and he/she.

AGORAPHOBIA:
A WOMAN'S PROBLEM?

Panic attacks can strike anyone at any time. But according to the latest research on the emotionally afflicted who go on to develop agoraphobia, more than sixty percent are women. The onset of this condition occurs most often between the ages of eighteen and thirty-four.

Several years ago one of my patients, "Karen," had an experience that she still recalls with tremendous horror. (Throughout this book, various cases will be presented. All names and identifying information have been changed to maintain the patient's confidentiality.) Karen felt scared and shaken because she did not know what was happening to her. Worse yet, she feared it would recur. When the attacks subsided, she called her doctor for help. After a cursory physical examination, he told her there seemed to be nothing wrong. Perhaps she was simply hyperventilating, he suggested, or was under too much stress. With her doctor's assurance that she was in excellent health, Karen attempted to resume her normal activities. Unfortunately, the attacks recurred and grew more frequent and severe. Before long, the only place that she felt safe was in her own home. Anytime she attempted to leave her home, the panicky feelings would begin. As she continued on her way, the attacks worsened until she felt she had no choice but to hurry back home. In time, she became agoraphobic, experiencing as many as ten to fifteen panic attacks a day.

Following several more visits to her doctor, and after assurances that nothing was wrong with her except perhaps a panic disorder (which apparently was supposed to make her feel better), she continued her daily routine, quietly dreading the next time she thought she'd lose her mind.

Then, one day, feeling unusually bold and adventurous, Karen found herself venturing along the freeway a little further from home than she'd allowed herself to go in some time. Suddenly, Karen noticed the scenery no longer looked familiar to her. As she anxiously looked around, searching for a landmark, she sensed the "It's-going-to-happen-again" feeling welling up inside. Her hands grew clammy. She clutched the steering wheel, her heart pounding. "I've got to get off the freeway," she told herself, but there were no off-ramps in sight. She veered into the right-hand lane. Waves of dizziness engulfed her. "Stay calm," she whispered to herself, while trembling all over. Then, after what seemed like an eternity, she spotted an exit ahead and sailed toward it gratefully.

Once off the freeway, she screeched to a halt at a service station to ask for directions home. She felt much too shaky to leave her car, so she just stared at the attendant until he eventually got the message and went over to her. As she started to speak, her voice seemed to boom loudly. But the attendant did not seem to notice. He gave Karen step-by-step directions for getting back on the freeway but she noticed a very strange thing. Once the word "freeway" emerged from his lips, she knew he'd been speaking English, but she realized she couldn't understand a thing he'd been saying! Her heart hammered so loudly that it drowned out his words.

Karen thanked him abruptly and swung out of the station. She decided to take safe side streets home instead. "Everything will be fine once I get home," she recited to herself. But, even with this reassurance, her heart was still racing wildly. As she hurried on, peering out at street signs until she found a familiar route, she recalled how the landscape appeared to take on an ominous gray pall. Houses and commercial buildings she knew so well somehow seemed "different." Suddenly nothing looked the same, and with this realization, Karen began to think she was truly losing her mind. As she continued on, she began to manufacture a terrible scenario. Karen imagined walking up to her door, seeing her husband and having him respond by saying, "Who are you? Do I know you?"

"For heaven's sake, John, it's me—your wife, Karen!"

"What kind of twisted joke are you trying to play on me, lady? My wife, Karen, died in a car crash four years ago! Now get out of here before I call the police!" This scenario may sound bizarre, but it is common among panic disorder sufferers.

Although scientists are not fully able to explain why more women than men are afflicted with agoraphobia, a number of theories have recently been advanced.

Traditionally, a woman with this condition may have found it easier to continue her daily routine. Clearly, male and female roles in the household have changed. Historically, however, many women have remained close to home, caring for the family. In these instances, if leaving home triggers anxiety, she can quickly return without disrupting too many of her normal activities. In contrast, a man with panic disorder probably cannot remain at home for long if he intends to hold on to his job. He might begin to drink—or drink more—to ease his anxieties and he may even attribute them to "job stress." But, since drinking merely masks anxiety, rather than relieving it, chances are he would continue to feel anxious. Still, he could not afford to develop agoraphobia—he could not let himself succumb to it—indeed, there is only a forty percent chance that he would.

The unusually high incidence of agoraphobia in women can also be linked to the different biochemistry of the two sexes. Men possess higher levels of the hormone testosterone, which is believed to contribute to aggressive behavior. Thus, if confronted by a threatening situation, a man is apt to stand his ground and fight. A panic attack does trigger this "fight-or-flight" response, and women, with their lower testosterone levels, are more likely to flee than to fight.

A third theory traces panic disorder to separation anxiety in childhood, a phenomenon that impacts more female than male children. At least girls are more apt to express this anxiety. Parents generally give them greater nurturing and reassurance, while boys are encouraged to be strong and to challenge their fears. A long separation from one or both parents, a perceived abandonment by either one, a sudden uprooting of the family, or even leaving home on one's own at a relatively young age— all of these can trigger separation anxiety. Because of their physiological makeup and social conditioning, girls are often less able to combat the symptoms of anxiety than are boys.

BIOLOGICAL ORIGINS OF ANXIETY
AND PANIC DISORDERS

Research findings indicate that genetics can play a key role in panic disorder. From early studies of patients diagnosed as having an "anxiety neurosis," experts found a higher correlation of the condition to exist in identical twins—possessing the same genetic blueprint—than in fraternal twins. More recently, a study conducted in Norway revealed the incidence of panic disorder to be five times greater in identical twins than in fraternal twins. In short, if either identical twin has a form of panic disorder, both are likely to have it. During the late 1800's, researchers James and Lang postulated that anxiety is a direct response to certain internal physical stimuli, such as increased heart rate and respiration. In other words, you experience deepening anxiety because your body has told your brain that you are anxious.

Similarly, in 1937, research studies found that persons with high levels of anxiety had more rapid heart rates than other people. Since then, other findings have reconfirmed this. Not only are their heart rates known to be faster, but persons with chronic anxiety generally are aware of their accelerated heart rates. In some cases, this awareness tends to reinforce their fear of having a heart attack, as well as their fear of dying.

Research also has found that the blood flow in the muscles of anxiety sufferers is substantially higher than in others, even when they are not experiencing high anxiety. In other words, "normal" people generally manifest high blood flow levels only when they are going through a great deal of stress. Anxiety sufferers often experience high blood flow even during resting states. As a result, their blood flow can more easily reach the highest levels of rapidity in a stressful cycle.

Further bearing out the Lang theory of internal stimuli, still other research studies have found that persons with panic disorder and agoraphobia tend to chronically hyperventilate more than other people.

These and other findings indicate a high rate of correlation between chronic anxiety and certain physiological functions of the body, which some scientists have come to regard as extremely significant in the understanding and treatment of panic disorders.

Why are physiological factors—other than increased heart rate, respiration and blood flow—directly linked to anxiety? The hormones known as *epinephrine* and *norepinephrine*, which generate states of arousal, are also known to be associated with anxiety. Research findings suggest that persons with generalized anxiety disorder have higher baseline levels of these two bodily hormones. It is not known yet, however, whether the same is true for individuals with panic disorder. But it is reasonable to assume that, if these hormone levels are elevated in persons with generalized anxiety, they could be higher in panic disorder sufferers as well.

Illness and Confinement

Many panic disorder sufferers have had an injury that required an extended period of confinement. Weeks or months of healing at home can make people more and more unaccustomed to the outside world. When they are finally able to venture out, they may find themselves momentarily overwhelmed by the sensory bombardment of traffic sounds, crowds, street noise, glaring lights, billboards and other stimuli. It is precisely at this time that they are most susceptible to a panic attack. If panic should strike, they are not apt to attribute it to having been housebound for so long. Instead, panic might seem to come from "out of the blue," a scary, almost paralyzing feeling that makes them feel vulnerable to still another attack.

Let us take a closer look at how certain physical conditions can contribute to or even cause anxiety disorders.

Mitral Valve Prolapse

Mitral valve prolapse has been found to be associated with panic disorder. This is a malfunction of the valves surrounding the heart that regulate blood flow. In most cases, it is not dangerous, and many persons have this condition without even knowing it. Some common symptoms of mitral valve prolapse include fatigue, chest pain, heart palpitations, difficulty in breathing, and fainting. A recent research study found a 50 percent incidence of mitral valve prolapse among persons who suffer panic attacks, suggesting that this condition and panic disorders are in some way related. However, research has also shown that it is unlikely that mitral valve prolapse actually causes panic attacks.

Hyperthyroidism

Hyperthyroidism is a condition in which the thyroid gland is overactive, causing the basal metabolism rate to be much higher than normal. Symptoms can include headaches, shakiness, and thoughts occurring much faster than they can be articulated (causing both rapid speech and impatience when listening to others); weight loss; and the inability to relax or to sleep, along with anxiety.

Premenstrual Syndrome (PMS)

PMS is another disorder of the endocrine system and therefore affects hormonal production. PMS is a condition in menstruating women, most often occurring 7-10 days prior to the onset of menstruation. The condition is attributed to an alteration in one's biochemistry initiated by the hormonal change associated with the menstrual cycle. Symptoms include water retention, shakiness, the inability to sleep or excessive sleep, mood swings, increased appetite and cravings for salty or sweet foods, along with anxiety.

Inner Ear Dysfunction and TMJ Syndrome

The term "inner ear" often means the cerebellum vestibular system (CVS). Some research suggests that this system may influence anxiety in humans.

Inner ear dysfunctions can have one or a number of causes, ranging from birth trauma to what is called temporomandibular joint syndrome (TMJ), or a dysfunction of the temporal mandibular joint. The condition is called a "syndrome" because it consists of a myriad of symptoms involving the joint, such as headaches, neck pain, lower back pain, a limited range of motion in the jaw, irritability, anxiety, dizziness, a feeling of "tightness" in the head, and sinus problems. One of the known signs of this disorder is chronic, unconscious grinding of the teeth, or "bruxing" during sleep.

TMJ syndrome is commonly treated by inserting an oral appliance or a "splint" to prevent this grinding activity. Chiropractic treatment has also been used effectively, as have acupressure, massage therapy and tranquilizers. In extreme cases, surgery may be necessary.

How can you know if you have TMJ syndrome? The answer may be as easy as a dental check-up. Chronic gum-chewers, pencil-biters and others whose jaws seem to be in almost constant motion all are likely TMJ syndrome candidates. In some cases, if the habit goes unchecked, it can contribute to the onset of panic symptoms.

How does inner ear dysfunction and TMJ syndrome provoke feelings of anxiety? Research has found that panic attacks are much more likely to strike when a person is fatigued. As one researcher explains it, "Your weakened powers of concentration may be incapable of adequately compensating for your CVS dysfunction."[1] It is this systemic failure that can give rise to feelings of anxiety.

Another explanation for this phenomenon is sensory overload. When one is fatigued, sensory stimuli such as lights flashing, horns honking and cars whizzing by can overwhelm the CVS, causing those who suffer from inner ear dysfunction to become confused and disoriented, even panicky.

This same dysfunction also can trigger dyslexia-related symptoms. Although they may not be as obvious as the transposition of letters or numbers, they can be equally disabling. These symptoms include spotty reading comprehension, frequent forgetfulness, poor spatial relationships and even motion sickness.

In most cases, CVS dysfunction can be diagnosed by a physician. Medication is the primary treatment. Although no drug has yet been developed specifically for treating CVS dysfunction, niacin, anti-motion drugs, and certain antihistamines and tranquilizers all seem to manage the symptoms effectively.

Fatigue

As we have just discussed, panic attacks are more likely to strike when a person is fatigued. But this doesn't refer to all people—not by any means. Feelings of fatigue in others merely cause irritability, mild confusion and a lack of motivation. But in persons with panic disorder, fatigue is apt to trigger feelings of weakness, dizziness and disorientation. This is an important point, for if the panic disorder sufferer feels disoriented and weak, an attack is almost sure to ensue. The reasons for this fatigue reaction pattern are not entirely clear. However, some scientists believe the adrenal glands become hyperactive as the body struggles to maintain a wakeful state and, as a result, produce excess adrenalin. While in normal persons this overproduction is rarely problematic, it does trigger anxiety-like symptoms which, for panic disorder individuals, can escalate into a panic attack.

Hypoglycemia

Hypoglycemia occurs when blood sugar levels dip below normal range. The glucose in blood sugar causes the body to secrete excessive epinephrine (adrenalin) in an attempt to stabilize glucose production. An abundance of adrenalin can be responsible for generating symptoms of shakiness, lightheadedness, excessive perspiration, headaches and heart palpitations. Many people suffer from hypoglycemia and are not aware that they have it. Hypoglycemia may develop as the result of certain drugs or the result of fasting, the inability to metabolize carbohydrates (reactive hypoglycemia) or may accompany diabetes.

A diagnosis of hypoglycemia is made by both a blood test and the symptoms reported by the patient. In some cases, an eight-hour glucose tolerance test is used, particularly if the diagnosis of diabetes is suspected.

Eating small meals every three to four hours that contain protein and reducing high intakes of sugar is recommended as treatment. However, if you are having a hypoglycemic episode, a glass of fruit juice or a piece of candy can boost your glucose level and quell symptoms.

Photophobia and Vision Problems

Hypersensitivity to sunlight has not been found to cause anxiety reactions in the general population. But among panic disorder persons, exposure to glaring sunlight or bright indoor lights can precipitate a panic attack. Thus, an attack that strikes in a supermarket or a shopping mall may actually have been triggered by fluorescent lights, whether alone or in combination with crowd noise, bright displays or other aggressive stimuli. For panic disorder sufferers who have any degree of *photophobia* (intolerance to bright light), wearing sunglasses inside stores and enclosed shopping malls can help to reduce the risk of an attack.

Faulty vision can also play a role in panic episodes. Among anxiety sufferers, even a minor change in visual perception or bodily sensations can be mistaken for the onset of a panic attack. The reason? During an actual attack, the person's vision often changes, growing somewhat blurred or distorted. Thus the hazy or distorted images that frequently result from poor vision can be interpreted as signaling a panic attack.

Yeast Infection

Research findings also indicate that yeast infections may contribute to anxiety symptoms. Yeast, explains Dr. William G. Crook, author of *The Yeast Connection*, is "a single-cell fungus that belongs to the vegetable kingdom. Like their cousins, molds, they live all around you."[2] Yeast germs are known to proliferate in the dark, warm hollows within the walls of the body's mucous membranes. The vagina and the intestinal tract are favorite breeding grounds of the yeast germ. Although there are many different varieties of yeast, the one that has recently received widespread attention as a source of potential illness is *candida albicans*.

Candida generally resides within the body in a healthy balance with other bacteria, unless the immune system becomes weakened. Antibiotics and cortisteroid medications can contribute to this weakening. Use of these drugs, in fact, may impair the immune system's functions so severely that the *Candida* begins to multiply at a staggering rate, destroying the "healthy" bacteria needed to ward off infections.

Along with continued use of antibiotics and cortisone, another factor that can contribute to runaway yeast growth within the body is a diet high in sugar, fat and yeast.

One common symptom of yeast infection is a sudden intolerance of tobacco smoke, perfumes and household chemical odors. Other warning signs are food allergies, persistent heartburn, bloating, gas, constipation or diarrhea, swollen joints, muscle weakness, numbness, feelings of lethargy or depression, recurring vaginal infections, nasal congestion, sore throat, chronic cough, fluid in the ears, blurred vision and the seeing of spots, feelings of unreality and a tightness in the chest and head. The most common symptoms of yeast infection happen to be symptoms characteristic of panic disorder. While *candida albicans* may not cause panic disorder, it can definitely intensify feelings of anxiety among panic sufferers.

Food Allergies

Being allergic to one or more foods is commonplace. We can recognize an allergic reaction to something we have eaten when the symptoms are immediate and obvious, such as nausea, sneezing or breaking out in a rash or hives. Some food allergy reactions, however, are not as apparent. These include an accelerated heart rate, blurred vision, headaches, a nasal discharge, swollen joints, dizziness, feelings of lethargy, sudden weight gain and even a craving for the very foods to which one is allergic. Feelings of anxiety are still another food allergy symptom. For many panic disorder individuals, eating food to which they are allergic can bring on a panic attack. The reason? Normally, the person does not realize that an accelerated heart rate, dizziness or blurred vision constitute an allergic reaction.

Instead, these symptoms are interpreted as signs of a panic attack. *Any small change in perception or bodily sensation will be interpreted as a cue for anxiety to erupt.* In other words, the person sets off a panic attack simply by believing that he or she is about to have one.

This is a cardinal point in understanding and treating panic disorder. *The sufferer's primary fear is of the panic attack itself and it is this fear which causes the attack's recurrence.* And since panic disorder sufferers have no clear-cut way to distinguish between real and seeming anxieties, a food allergy reaction that raises anxiety feelings is almost sure to set off a panic attack.

Some of the common food substances known to provoke allergic reactions are citrus fruit, potatoes, tuna, shellfish, dairy products, wheat, soy, corn, sugar, artificial sweeteners and colorings, nitrates, monosodium glutamate, coffee and alcoholic beverages. Also worth noting is that many persons infected with *candida albicans* go on to develop food allergies.

Sugar, Caffeine and Nicotine

Use of sugar, caffeine or nicotine is known to increase the heart rate. Caffeine and nicotine are stimulants and can also affect the user's basal metabolism. Most panic disorder sufferers quickly discover on their own that drinking caffeinated coffee, tea or soft drinks can bring on an attack. However, they are often unaware of the relationship between panic attacks and smoking or sugar intake.

Dehydration

Dehydration is caused by a deficiency of water in the body. Certain diseases can cause dehydration, such as Addison's disease, chronic diarrhea associated with gastrointestinal disease, and Diabetes Mellitus. Excessive exposure to heat without adequate fluid intake or medications such as diuretics or those used to treat the HIV virus can also cause dehydration. The condition causes the blood pressure to drop dramatically upon rising (orthostatic hypotension), producing dizziness, disorientation, the feelings of faintness, and in severe cases, fainting. Treatment focuses on first identifying the cause of the dehydration. Once this is established and treated accordingly, the body needs to be rehydrated. If the symptoms of dehydration are mild, abundant fluid intake of a beverage containing high concentrations of sodium may be sufficient. If the symptoms are more severe, hospitalization may be required so that electrolytes can be evaluated and supplied intravenously.

Environmental Allergies

Being allergic to one or more pollutants in the environment can bring on symptoms similar to those of food allergies. Many panic disorder patients report that their anxieties soar when they are driving in heavy traffic, possibly because they feel "trapped." But another reason can be their allergic reaction to carbon monoxide fumes, which build to peak concentrations in gridlocked traffic. As noted earlier, when a person with panic disorder mistakes the common symptoms of an allergic reaction for anxiety feelings—namely, an increased heart rate, dizziness and blurred vision—a panic attack is almost sure to ensue.

Carbon monoxide is but one of hundreds of chemical substances that can provoke allergic reactions. Many of these chemical compounds are found in the workplace, and they often generate allergy symptoms without the person even knowing it. Some buildings, particularly those under construction, contain chemical substances that can trigger allergic reactions in people who are sensitive to these toxins. Those with candida albicans infections often are unable to tolerate certain environmental pollutants as well. These include pollutants from shampoos, moisturizers, hair spray and room deodorizers. There are various illnesses and medications which can cause or exacerbate anxiety symptoms. A detailed list of these illnesses and drugs are delineated on Tables 1.1 and 1.2.

From this, we can see that anxiety disorders—long regarded as untreatable neuroses—actually have their roots in our heredity, environment, medical history, nutritional habits, drug use, and even—as shown by their link to TMJ syndrome—to how we react to inner stress. Once the roots manifest themselves in

Table 1.1 ■■■

MEDICAL CONDITIONS ASSOCIATED WITH
ANXIETY/DEPRESSION

ILLNESS	SYSTEM	SYMPTOMS
Sleep Apnea	Neurological	Startled awakening with gasping, headache, tachycardia, poor concentration
Sinusitis	Ear, nose, throat	Headache, malaise, blurred vision, dizziness, head feels full, eye pain, fever, and chills
Orthostatic Hypotension	Blood pressure	Dizziness upon standing, feeling faint or fainting, rapid pulse, weakness, light-headedness
Multiple Sclerosis	Neurological	Weakness, visual disturbances, depression and anxiety, symptoms worsen with excessive heat, impaired judgment, poor concentration, weakness and tingling in limbs, vertigo
Cardiovascular		Feeling faint or faint-disorders, dizziness, palpitations, tachycardia, shortness of breath, chest pain, light-headedness, weakness, fatigue, anxiety
Chronic Fatigue Syndrome	Viral	Inability to concentrate, memory impairment, dizziness, weakness, extreme fatigue, heart palpitations, shortness of breath, visual disturbances, exercise worsens symptoms, memory impairment

Continued on next page

ILLNESS	SYSTEM	SYMPTOMS
Lyme Disease	Bacterial	Malaise, memory impairment, vomiting, nausea, palpitations, headache, stiff neck, mild cardiac abnormalities, panic attacks, obsessive-compulsive behaviors
Meniere's Syndrome	Neurological	Severe dizziness, nausea, vomiting, heavy sweating, rapid eye oscillation, fainting, panic attacks
Menopause	Hormonal	Dizziness, hot flashes, anxiety, sleeplessness, irritability, forgetfulness, fatigue, vague bodily sensations
Adrenal Insufficiency (Addison's Disease)	Endocrine	Weakness, fatigue, dizziness, fainting, nausea, vomiting, shortness of breath, palpitations, weight loss, loss of appetite
Migraine	Head/Vascular	Excessive sweating, nausea, vomiting, visual disturbances, numbing and tingling of the extremities, photophobia, slowed thinking, head pain
Diabetes Mellitus	Endocrine	Excessive thirst, dizziness, rapid pulse, weakness, fatigue, blurred vision, poor coordination, poor concentration, light-headedness, fainting, panic attacks
Hyperthyroidism	Endocrine	Diarrhea, headaches, weakness, palpitations, tremors, panic attacks, excessive perspiration, shortness of breath

Table 1.2

MEDICATIONS AND OTHER SUBSTANCES ASSOCIATED WITH ANXIETY/DEPRESSION

TYPE	INDICATIONS
Diuretics	Hypertension, water retention
Cortisone	Inflammation for a wide variety of conditions including rashes, autoimmune diseases, asthma, joint swelling, allergies, cancer, AIDS
Hormones	Hypothyroidism, hysterectomy, menopause, male impotence, birth control
Bronchodilators	Lung cancer, emphysema, asthma, upper respiratory infections and allergies
Antihistamines and Decongestants (particularly those containing pseudo-ephedrine)	Allergies, colds, sinus infections
Novocaine, Lido-Caine	Local anesthetics for dental procedures
Pain Killers (Ultrum, Vicoden)	Pain management
Compazine	Vomiting, severe nausea
Epinephrine Injection	Anaphylaxis, allergies, rash, cardiac disturb-ances
Stimulants (Ritilin, Cyclert, Dexadrine, Fenfluramine [Pondimine])	Treatment for attention deficit disorder, depression, weight loss
Paradoxical reactions to an abrupt withdrawal from sedatives, tranquilizers	Anxiety, insomnia, chronic stomach pain
Antibiotics	Bacterial and fungal infections
Recreational Drugs (Crystal Methadrine, Ecstacy, PCP, LSD, Crack/Cocaine, Alcohol, Marijuana)	Varied
Natural Substances (Tea, Coffee, Aspartame, Herbs—Ginko biloba, Ginseng, Ma-haung/Ephedra)	Energy, memory enhancement, weight loss

the form of an attack, panic disorders are reinforced and perpetuated by: 1) our fear that they will recur and 2) the tendency to mistake physiological or emotional stimuli for new, dangerous anxiety, and then to overreact and invite another panic attack.

Anxiety disorders are treatable. But they continue to victimize millions of people who lack access to important information regarding assessment and treatment. The following pages enumerate the symptoms associated with certain anxiety disorders. It is important to recognize that the following criterion have been delineated to assist you, they are *not* designed to replace an evaluation by a mental health professional.

SELF ASSESSMENT:
GLOSSARY OF ANXIETY SYMPTOMS

Panic Attack

- Shortness of breath or a "smothering" sensation
- Dizziness, faintness, or feelings of unsteadiness
- Palpitations or an accelerated heartbeat
- Trembling or shaking
- Sweating or having clammy hands
- A choking sensation
- Nausea or abdominal discomfort
- Feelings of being unreal
- Numbness or tingling sensations
- "Hot flashes" or chills
- Chest pain or discomfort
- Fear of going crazy or out of control
- Fear of dying

If you have experienced at least *four* of these thirteen symptoms, you have had a panic attack. If the attack recurred for at least one month, chances are you have a form of panic disorder.

Agoraphobia

If you are somewhat convinced you have a panic disorder, the next step is to determine which of the two subtypes of panic disorder you are experiencing—the type with agoraphobia or without agoraphobia. Panic disorder afflicts both men and women in roughly equal numbers. But over sixty percent of the panic disorder sufferers who develop agoraphobia are *women*.

Agoraphobia means that panic attacks intensify in both frequency and severity as the individual gets further away from home. In panic attacks *without* agoraphobia, the distance from home plays no discernible role in heightening the anxiety. The key difference between these two types of panic disorder, then, are 1) what sets off the anxiety and 2) how it manifests itself.

- Do you feel uncomfortable when you're far away from home?
- Do you find excuses not to go too far away from home?
- Do you avoid going into markets, shopping malls, theatres, doctors' offices and other buildings because they make you anxious?
- Do you wait until you can go with a friend to these places, and do you find it makes you less anxious when you do?

If you feel unable to relate to the symptoms described above, it may be because you have a panic disorder without agoraphobia. Or, you could be experiencing agoraphobia without ever having had a panic attack!

Agoraphobia Without a History of Panic Attacks

People who have this type of disorder may never have suffered a panic attack, yet tend to feel jittery or uneasy if they venture far from home. They eventually come to fear the onset of these anxieties. Yet, many of these persons are totally unaware of their condition. Instead, they believe they merely "choose" to stay home or "prefer to go places" with their spouse or friends rather than on their own.

Social Phobia

This condition is a persistent fear of one or more social situations in which a person may be exposed to unusual scrutiny by others. People who suffer this disorder fear they might do or say things in a social setting that will embarrass or even humiliate them. Among the foremost questions to be posed of this potential sufferer are:

- Do you find yourself unable to continue while speaking in public?
- Do you start choking on food when eating in front of others?
- Do you become unable to urinate in a public lavatory?
- Does your hand tremble when writing in the presence of others?
- Do you become unable to answer questions when asked?
- Do you catch yourself saying or doing things that offend others?

Social phobics tend to avoid interacting with other people for much the same reason that agoraphobics avoid the confinement of crowds. The similarity between social phobia and agoraphobia goes even deeper. The findings of one recent research study show that many housebound agoraphobics actually are social phobics.

Phobias

A phobia is an irrational fear of a nonthreatening object, place or situation. If a woman who lives alone regularly checks to make sure her doors and windows are locked because she fears an intruder might enter her home and harm her, she does not necessarily have a phobia. Since one out of three women in our society are rape victims, her fear is probably not unwarranted. However, if this same woman continually patrolled her doors and windows with a can of insecticide, fearing a spider might enter, she probably has a phobia—specifically, *arachnophobia.* Most spiders, although not particularly attractive, are not a threat to her survival. Of course, if her home were teeming with black widow spiders, her behavior would be a legitimate response to a potentially dangerous situation.

Phobias develop for a variety of reasons. Panic disorder with agoraphobia frequently includes certain phobias such as *claustrophobia* (fear of small, enclosed spaces), *acrophobia* (fear of heights) and even freeway phobia. Panic disorder is *not* likely to include narrower, more specialized fears that center on a single source of dread, such as germs, insects or birds.

Posttraumatic Stress Disorder (PTSD)

The condition known as Posttraumatic Stress Disorder often occurs in people who have experienced a trauma such as an auto accident, witnessing or being the victim of a violent crime, or surviving a natural disaster. Although many symptoms of PTSD resemble those of panic disorder, it is important to recognize the differences between these conditions.

1. Do you experience recurrent and intrusive recollections of the event?

2. Do you have recurrent dreams of the event?

3. Do you suddenly act or feel as if the traumatic event were recurring (including a sense of reliving the experience, illusions, hallucinations or flashbacks) upon, say, awakening or when intoxicated?

4. Do you experience intense psychological stress when exposed to any situations that symbolize or represent an aspect of the traumatic event, including anniversaries of the trauma?

5. Do you persistently avoid situations associated with the trauma or a numbing of your general responsiveness, as indicated by at least *three* of the following:

A. Do you make efforts to avoid thoughts or feelings associated with the trauma?

B. Do you make efforts to avoid activities or situations that arouse recollections of the trauma?

C. Do you have an inability to recall an important aspect of the trauma?

D. Do you have a markedly diminished interest in significant activities?

E. Do you have feelings of detachment or estrangement from others?

F. Do you have restricted emotions (e.g., the inability to have loving feelings)?

G. Do you sense a shortened future (e.g., you do not expect to have a career, marriage or children, or a very long life)?

6.   Do you have persistent symptoms of increased arousal (not present before the trauma) as indicated by at least all of the following:

A. Difficulty falling or staying asleep?

B. Psychological reactivity on encountering situations that symbolize or resemble an aspect of the traumatic event (e.g., a woman who was raped in an elevator breaks out in a sweat when entering any elevator).

C. Being disturbed by these combined symptoms for at least *one* month.

Not all persons who have experienced trauma go on to develop posttraumatic stress disorder. Even some of those who do may not develop the first symptoms until six months or so after the trauma. When this occurs, it is called a "delayed onset." Now that we have seen why PTSD is sometimes mistaken for a panic disorder, let's take a look at another condition that's even more frequently misdiagnosed.

Generalized Anxiety Disorder (GAD)

The condition known as generalized anxiety disorder is often confused with panic disorder, and for good reason. If you scan the list of GAD symptoms that follow, you'll see how similar they are to panic disorder symptoms. The key difference between these conditions, though, is the frequency, intensity and duration of anxiety episodes. In addition, persons who suffer from generalized anxiety disorder tend to be focused on the fear of something happening to a loved one, or on an *overconcern* about work relationship, or health. Their anxieties are more or less constant, although certain stressors can exacerbate them. Achieving relief, or an easing, of these symptoms does not require avoiding or withdrawing from a given situation.

In addition, they do not experience panic attacks. Rather, they usually feel a continuous and pervasive undercurrent of fear. GAD does not develop into agoraphobia. Does this description give you reason to believe that you may have GAD? Read through the list of GAD symptoms to see if they apply.

    1.   Do you experience continuous unrealistic anxiety and worry about two or more life situations? For example, do you worry about possible harm coming to your child (who is in no apparent danger), and worry about job loss (without good reason) for a period of six or more months?

    2.   Do you have at least *six* of the following symptoms?
       A. trembling, twitching or feeling shaky
       B. muscle tension, aches or soreness
       C. restlessness
       D. strong fatigue and depression
       E. shortness of breath or "smothering" sensations
       F. palpitations or an accelerated heart rate
       G. sweating or having cold, clammy hands
       H. dry mouth
       I. dizziness or lightheadedness
       J. nausea, diarrhea or abdominal distress
       K. hot flashes" or chills
       L. frequent urination
       M. trouble swallowing or a "lump in the throat"
       N. feelings of being keyed up or on edge
       O. exaggerated startle response
       P. difficulty concentrating or having your "mind go blank"

If you have answered yes to at least · three of these symptoms and have been experiencing them for at least six months, you may have GAD.

Obsessive-Compulsive Disorder

Obsessive-Compulsive Disorder afflicts nearly five million

Americans. The symptoms of OCD can be broken down into two distinct features, obsessions and compulsions. Obsessions are unwanted and intrusive thoughts that occur repeatedly. Compulsions are the behaviors initiated by those thoughts which are performed in an attempt to minimize anxiety. Do you have obsessions that center around the following concerns?

- Dirt and contamination?
- Inappropriate sexual themes?
- Need to arrange objects in a particular manner?
- Hoarding?
- Religious obsessions?
- Illogical obsessions?
- Fear of causing harm to others?
- Are you superstitious?

Do you act out ritualistic behaviors with regard to the following?

- Cleaning?
- Checking repeatedly (oven is turned off, doors locked, etc.)?
- An excessive desire to ask someone something or confess something to someone?
- Counting?
- Touching?
- Overwhelming need to make lists?
- Asking repeatedly for approval from others?
- Staring or blinking?
- Compulsive shopping?
- Nail biting?
- Hair pulling?
- Excessive eating or drinking?

Obsessive-Compulsive Disorder is frequently accompanied by depression. Similar to GAD, it is often misdiagnosed and even confused with GAD. If you engage in these obsessions and compulsions for at least an hour every day and they impair your social, or occupational functioning, you may have O.C.D. The symptoms range from mild to severe. O.C.D. should not be confused with Obsessive Compulsive Personality Disorder, characterized by rigid behaviors which are not caused by an anxiety disorder.

Adjustment Disorder

Experiencing frequent bouts of nervousness or fear doesn't necessarily mean one has an anxiety disorder. Unexpected events that occur in our lives and the major adjustments they sometimes force on us can also trigger anxieties. Making the required changes generally relieves these feelings. But if we resist or are unable to cope with change, our anxieties can intensify and even precipitate phobic behavior. In clinical terms, this is known as an Adjustment Disorder with Anxious Mood. If you are currently in a period of transition, faced with making decisions that seem scary or more than you can handle, this may explain why you are feeling as you do. But your condition probably is not an anxiety disorder. Nonetheless, you can still benefit from the tools and techniques discussed in the following chapters.

Anxiety Disorder Due to a Medical Condition

Until recently, the psychiatric community classified anxiety as a psychological disorder stemming from a psychological cause.

In 1994, the American Psychiatric Association published the DSM IV and the diagnostic criteria included a new classification labeled, "Anxiety Disorder Due To A Medical Condition." The same classification now exists for mood disorders as well. The inclusion of these categories behind-hand as they may be, deserve celebration. Far too many anxiety sufferers have had their symptoms minimized by both mental health care providers and physicians alike. At last, the validity of seeking medical evaluation for symptoms of anxiety has been legitimated.

If you suffer from chronic illness or pain and/or take certain medications on an ongoing basis, your anxiety may be attributable to your medical condition or your medicines. It is therefore *always* recommended that you receive a full medical checkup before assuming that your symptoms are "all in your head."

The anxiety arising from a medical condition may cause:

1. Generalized anxiety
2. Panic attacks
3. Obsessive-compulsive behaviors.

One example of how a medical condition can cause symptoms of anxiety is the following case:

Robert sought treatment at the Institute for panic attacks. Robert reported that the onset of his attacks coincided with a long plane ride while he was experiencing gastrointestinal distress. On the plane, he began to feel trapped, causing his anxiety to worsen.

The panic attacks continued to occur long after his trip and at various places, particularly those where a restroom was not immediately accessible. Robert's gastrointestinal symptoms worsened along with his anxiety.

After several weeks of severe diarrhea and cramping, Robert visited a specialist. The physician did a GI workup but was unable to provide a diagnosis. The physician suggested that the symptoms were a result of Robert's anxiety and recommended antidepressant medication. Robert's symptoms did not improve and the medication exacerbated his gastrointestinal complaints.

For six months, Robert endured chronic diarrhea, cramping and a great deal of anxiety. He visited another specialist who also implied that his symptoms were anxiety related.

Robert's occupation demanded that he fly frequently. The panic attacks grew so severe that not only could he no longer fly but he became agoraphobic and had to take a medical leave from work.

When Robert entered treatment, he initially presented himself as someone with a panic disorder. However, after careful evaluation of his history, I reserved the diagnosis of panic disorder and recommended further medical evaluation. Robert finally located a specialist who knew what questions to ask.

After it was ascertained that his symptoms developed subsequent to a trip in South America, the doctor suspected that Robert had a parasite. His physician explained that parasites are often difficult to isolate, even with the most sophisticated testing. He prescribed high doses of a medication specifically for a parasitic infection and within a few weeks, Robert's gastrointestinal symptoms started to improve, as did his anxiety.

Robert was diagnosed with an, Anxiety Disorder Due to Infectious Diarrhea. Psychotherapy focused on reinforcing that his anxiety was medically based. Cognitive therapy and hypnosis assisted that process and within a few months, Robert no longer suffered from anxiety or panic attacks. In fact, the last time I heard from him, he was taking flying lessons!

Chapter 2

SPECIAL ISSUES ASSOCIATED WITH PANIC DISORDER

PREGNANCY

When a woman has a panic disorder and becomes pregnant, there are two factors that can aggravate her condition. First and foremost is drug use. Medications such as Valium, Zanax, Ativan, and other benzodiazepines have been reported in some rare circumstance to complicate pregnancy cases, to cause the baby to be born addicted. The mother would be well advised to consult a physician in this matter.

The second factor concerns the hormonal changes associated with various stages of pregnancy that can exaggerate the fear of being trapped. Imagine yourself in a windowless hospital room under bright lights, feeling great pain and knowing there is no escape. Delivering a baby is a commitment from which there is no turning back, no running toward the safety of your own home. This realization can evoke terror in many panic disorder sufferers, all the more reason for you to take extra care in avoiding pregnancy until appropriate. "Oh no, but I'm already pregnant!" you may say. Relax. This book, along with the advice of your physician, can help you to withdraw from medication without becoming debilitated by anxiety. If you are currently taking an antidepressant—Prozac, Imipramine, Zoloft, Desyrel, Paxil, or others—you may also want to speak with your physician or a genetic counselor about the possible side effects it could have on the fetus. Should you decide to reduce or to eliminate your medication, see your physician. Only do so under his or her supervision. If you are on medication and wish to become pregnant or are pregnant, do not scare yourself unnecessarily. This book is designed to help people overcome anxiety without drugs when applicable.

FUNCTIONAL AGORAPHOBIA

Gastrointestinal Disease and Agoraphobia

For most of us, going to the bathroom is nothing to fear. Crohn's disease, Irritable Bowel Syndrome, and Ulcerative Colitis are digestive maladies affecting the bowels in such a way that going to the bathroom anywhere but in one's own home can be most embarrassing, even terrifying. Diarrhea, gas discomfort and foul gas expulsions are typical symptoms. They often contribute to a special kind of agoraphobia. People who suffer from these symptoms will often decline invitations to parties, theaters, shopping malls, even to a friend's home for fear that they may need to use the bathroom. This problem is cause enough for concern, but if it exists in conjunction with a panic disorder, it can be devastating.

You may not have a gastrointestinal disease, yet every time you become anxious, diarrhea strikes. This is because diarrhea can be a symptom of panic disorder. Whether you suffer from intestinal problems or get attacks of diarrhea from the panic, the emotional impact is similar.

This book will help you manage and eventually overcome anxiety associated with panic disorder. As for the embarrassment stemming from bowel disturbance, it is critical that you come to terms with this problem and resign yourself to using a public restroom (without unnecessary embarrassment). You can use matches, perfumes, and the practice of flushing the toilet constantly to avoid any embarrassing sounds or odors you may create. Most of all, realize that everyone experiences diarrhea occasionally from eating improperly or from illness. You do not have to feel as though there is a bright spotlight over your bathroom stall and a loud booming voice announcing that you and only you are contaminating the whole restroom with your odor. I assure you that no one will glare and point at you when you leave your stall. If you cannot resolve your fear of going to the bathroom away from home, you may want to join a support group such as those affiliated with the Crohn's and Colitis Foundation of America (CCFA). There is an extensive resource list, including the phone number of the CCFA, at the end of this book.

Urinary Urgency

One in three individuals will experience some type of problem with maintaining bladder control. The majority of individuals afflicted are women. Urinary urgency can be the result of infections, inflammation of the bladder, weak muscles, endometriosis, lupus, tumors, hormonal imbalances, interstitial cystitis, and a host of other maladies, some of which are more responsive to treatment than others.

The degree and frequency of symptoms vary with the etiology of the disease. By and large, the common thread of concern is that the individual will need to urinate and will be unable to locate a restroom quickly.

Often, a complicating factor is the pain that may accompany the symptoms of urgency. Moreover, many women have been inadequately evaluated by their physicians. I have treated several clients who, once they made the disclosure that they had an anxiety disorder to their doctors, were told that their urgency and pain were the result of obsessive thinking. Only after pursuing specialist upon specialist did these individuals discover that a medical condition was actually responsible for their symptoms.

If you suffer from urinary urgency and your doctor has not been able to identify a cause and has suggested that your symptoms are psychosomatic, you would be well advised to consult another physician, perhaps a different type of specialist, such as a gynecologist. If it appears that you will need to accept your condition as a symptom that may persist for sometime, you cannot afford to allow it to make you a shut-in. Ask your doctor about certain medications which can minimize some of the physical sensations. In addition, do not let yourself succumb to feelings of embarrassment that will eventually dictate your lifestyle. If you are overconcerned with access to a restroom, a pattern of anxiety and avoidance will surely ensue.

Paruresis (Bashful Bladder Syndrome)

Paruresis, or the anxiety associated with urinating in a public lavatory, is a symptom of social phobia. Paruresis afflicts males and females equally. However, males are often more impacted by the symptoms because their restrooms are designed differently. From the moment they enter a restroom, males are confronted by their fear in a more direct way.

While women have the luxury of anonymity in a stall and can wait until they are alone to urinate, a male may not always have access to a stall. The harder he tries to relieve himself in the presence of others, the more anxiety it creates. The greater the anxiety, the more aware he is that others are noticing he is unable to urinate. It becomes a vicious cycle. The anxiety limits the flow of urine which only adds pressure to void in the presence of others, increasing further anxiety. Soon, no place is safe: the work place, restaurants, health clubs, movie theaters, parties. As you might suspect, the paruretic learns to plan his activities well in advance in order to avoid restrooms as much as possible. Eventually, he exists within his own agoraphobic comfort zone.

The treatment for paruresis is usually a combination of exposure therapy and certain antidepressant medications. Exposure therapy is usually done with a therapist of the same gender who can accompany the paruretic into public places. The therapist initially remains at a great distance from the client and with each trip to a public restroom maintains less and less distance. Eventually, the client is able to relieve himself with the therapist in closer proximity. Before pursuing exposure therapy, it is always advisable to visit a physician, preferably a urologist, to rule out any medical condition. Once it has been determined that symptoms are not associated with a medical problem, one can commence with the exposure therapy, either with a friend who can act as co-therapist or alone.

Whether you are embarking on this exercise alone or with the help of a co-therapist your goal should be achieved incrementally. Choose the most non-threatening circumstances first. For example, go into a restroom with the least amount of traffic, using the toilet in the stall and waiting until there is only one person in the lavatory. Try this again on another day until there are two people, then three. Venture out to other restrooms and do the same thing. Eventually, you should be ready to stand at a urinal alone. Before attempting to void, breathe deeply and slowly. In *this* setting, you are insignificant. Do not delude yourself into believing that the sound of your urine is of any importance to anyone but you. The only goal others have when they enter the restroom is to relieve themselves as quickly as possible. In many respects, to them you are invisible. As you remind yourself that your self-consciousness is without merit and, if you practice exposure therapy consistently, your anxiety will diminish.

TERMINAL AND CATASTROPHIC ILLNESS AND THE FEAR OF DYING

The most prominent feature of panic disorder is an irrational fear of dying and/or of going insane. The psychotherapist spends many sessions with clients helping them to accept the fact that they are probably in good health and are not going to die in the imminent future. But what about survivors of catastrophic illness or of terminal disease?

As such a survivor, you may have developed a panic disorder subsequent to your diagnosis, and some anxiety is certainly a normal reaction. Conversely, perhaps you had been troubled by a panic disorder for several years and were then diagnosed with a serious illness. In either case, if you follow the step-by-step instructions outlined later in this book, you can overcome your anxiety.

It is important that you are aware that although anxiety is a perfectly appropriate response to a serious disease, symptoms can worsen from the side effects of certain medications. Treatment of cancer and AIDS, for example, frequently involves the use of prednisone (a steroid) which, in large doses, can affect one's ability to sleep—as well as induce a feeling of euphoria. Negative side effects include anxiety and irritability. If you have lung cancer, you may be taking bronchodilators to help you breathe more easily. This can also promote nervousness and/or anxiety. It may be necessary to continue taking medication regardless of its unpleasant side effects, but if you are aware that much of your panic stems from these chemicals, you will probably be less concerned about your anxiety. If you suffer from catastrophic disease or a terminal illness, find a support group. If, however, you are agoraphobic, it is vital that you make contact with an organization representing those who suffer from your disease.

LOVE RELATIONSHIPS

Panic attacks can make you feel as though you are being divorced from reality by an invisible barrier of fear. The presence of someone familiar to you can ground you in the "real" world—but the person can also become, in a sense, the keeper of your mind. You may slowly become convinced that, as long as he/she is with you, you will be okay. He/she will make the decisions for you if you cannot, or will drive the car when you cannot, or will make sure you are always "safe." This erroneous belief has caused the partners of panic disorder sufferers to feel an enormous sense of responsibility for the health and welfare of the other. Eventually, the demands may be so great that the marriage or relationship cannot endure the stress and it dissolves. The panic disorder sufferer's worst nightmare—to be left alone forever in an agoraphobic hell— may indeed come true.

It is not my intention to scare you into thinking that your relationship is doomed. However, you should be aware of the potential consequences of remaining over reliant on your partner. Living within a limited radius over an extended period of time can begin to seem "normal." Often, the panic disorder sufferer can become complacent and with someone on whom she can be dependent, loses motivation to challenge herself. Do not allow yourself to fall into this trap.

Eventually, your relationship could degenerate, particularly in cases of severe agoraphobia. Your partner may love you very deeply, but taking care of someone with a severe panic disorder for an extended period of time is extremely difficult.

Thus, it may be necessary for you to ask your partner how he feels about this disorder and to make it clear that you have a renewed determination to overcome your problem. This means that you will practice the steps outlined in this book to the best of your ability. It is up to your partner to support you in this effort. It is not your partner's responsibility, however, to see to it that you finish this book and that you make progress. That responsibility is yours alone.

SUICIDE

Really, it has nothing to do with you.
I'm just tired of waking up with a crippled body and a bent mind.
You know how sometimes the sun's too bright—and you can't go out alone because when the light turns red you suddenly disappear?
I have you to remind me that I'm not invisible.

But you leave for another planet in two weeks and my mind
will be packed in your suitcase.
I hate needing you; euthanasia cures insanity.
Please don't look at me that way.
Just help me pull the trigger and I'll love you forever.[3]

Adults with panic disorder are 18 times more likely to have attempted suicide or thought about it than adults with no other mental illness. The implications of this statistic are staggering. But if you suffer from panic disorder, this information may not seem that surprising.

As I mentioned earlier, a prominent symptom of panic disorder is the fear of dying. Nonetheless, many sufferers engage in behavior that can result in the very thing they fear the most—death. This is not as illogical as it may seem. Panic attacks occur because you fear the fear. The by-products of this rush of fear are physical symptoms that are interpreted as signals to you that you are dying. Your heart pounds furiously, your chest constricts, and the adrenalin coursing through your body suggests to your mind that death must indeed be approaching. Living with the dread of these attacks on a daily basis wears you down to such a fragile state that suicide may appear to be a perfectly rational way to escape the feeling of being eternally trapped in a constant state of terror.

If you are reading this book because someone you love has a panic disorder, encourage the person to get help immediately. Do not take their symptoms lightly. If you suffer from panic disorder and suicide has seemed to be your only viable option, you need to enlist the services of a mental health provider immediately! Do not allow embarrassment or feelings of hopelessness to prevent you from getting help. Take heart. You are not alone and *you can overcome your fear.*

The poem you read was written by a former client who was agoraphobic. She actually prayed that she would have the courage to take her own life. She never thought her fear would allow her to live a normal life. Now, after years of traveling around the world, she is grateful that she did not give up. You can do it, too. The following chapters will help you take your first step.

SELF-DISCLOSURE

What Do I Tell My Children?
    Disclosing your anxiety disorder to an adult has benefits and risks. The benefits are obvious. You can liberate yourself from feelings of shame and also allow yourself to be given support, encouragement and help. The risk is that certain people may not be capable of understanding the scope of your symptoms and judge you as someone who is "emotionally unstable." A perception such as this is certainly not the kind of attitude any one of us wishes to encounter. Still, this kind of harsh disapproval, as uncomfortable as it may be, cannot harm you. Overall, sharing your symptoms with adults who care about you and offering to educate them about your disease often enriches relationships and can increase self-esteem by eliminating the barriers that once concealed your deep, dark secret of anxiety.
    But what about sharing this information with your child? The benefits and risks are not the same. Your child is not capable of providing you with the same emotional support as an adult, nor should this be expected. The question posed is not how you can benefit from your self-disclosure to your child, but rather what are the possible ramifications of such an action?
    Try to imagine that you are eight years old and your mother tells you she cannot take you to a soccer game because she has a disease which is hereditary and causes her to feel as if she is losing her mind. She proceeds to elaborate on the details of the various physiological and psychological symptoms associated with a panic episode. Most likely, you would feel very frightened that your mother, someone who you rely upon to take care of you, appears to have lost control over her faculties. As an eight year old, you cannot understand the complexities of an anxiety disorder. Your interpretation of your

mother's description of her panic attacks and her subsequent limitations may cause you to believe that she is in fact crazy.

Additionally, there are other factors to consider. Panic disorder is hereditary and new studies confirm that Generalized Anxiety Disorder also has a genetic component as well. Informally, this predisposition is referred to as the "worry gene." This could mean your child may have a potential to develop an anxiety disorder. If your child is struggling with an existing anxiety disorder (of which you are unaware), particularly if it is a generalized anxiety disorder, your child may worry excessively when given too much information. Stating words such as disease, hereditary, etc. can also suggest that your child may inevitably develop the same symptoms, a concern that can escalate into excessive anxiety as the child matures.

Conversely, deliberately withholding information from your child, when it is obvious there is something wrong, can create confusion and anxiety as well. Understand that there is no easy answer. Experts often disagree on how much or how little information should be discussed. However, there are certain parameters of dialogue to consider. The following guidelines may be helpful in determining how and what you communicate with your child.

1. How old is your child?

2. Has your child exhibited significant symptoms of separation anxiety or consistently expressed the fear that you may be in danger of being harmed?

3. To what degree has your child been exposed to your panic symptoms while they were occurring and what has already been communicated by you or other family members?

4. Has your child expressed the desire to know? Are the questions probing or vague?

The age of your child is particularly significant. Clearly, a fifteen year old is capable of understanding more sophisticated explanations than a four year old. Still, you would want to be very cautious about not only the content of your communication but your attitude about it as well. Take into account the possibility that your child may be very suggestible, particularly because of the genetic predisposition to an anxiety disorder. Try to feel the pulse of his/her reactions. By and large, the less details you offer, the less worry you will generate. The following example may help in knowing how to respond to your child.

Dylan (seven years old): Mommy, how come you haven't been taking me to school lately?

Mom: Well, Dylan, I have been getting a little dizzy when I drive lately and the doctor wants me to rest so I can get better.

Dylan: Why do you get dizzy? Are you sick?

Mom: No, Honey, not really. The doctor thinks that I'm perfectly fine but I've been very busy and need to slow down. So, when I'm too active, my body tells me it is time to rest. Don't worry, the doctor knows exactly how to help me. But I may need a little time to heal. So, for a while, your Grandmother or Daddy or other people might be driving you places, just until I feel better again.

When Dylan's inquiry abates, this is an indication that he is probably satisfied with your response. If he persists with investigating further, you may need to emphasize that you are not seriously ill and that the doctor is helping you to recover. Providing additional information is not necessary.

But what if your child is a teenager, should you disclose more?

Once again, you will want to familiarize yourself with the guidelines for self-disclosure. You should also be aware of your attitude *about* your situation and the type of relationship you have with your teenager. Your reply can reveal more information without being too specific. You may wish to add that when you get dizzy, you become frightened and, with the help of your doctor or psychotherapist, you are learning not to be afraid. It is not necessary to provide a label for your symptoms. Each situation is different. If your teenager indicates he would like you to be more explicit and you feel that he will be able to accept knowing more details, then disclose little by little and monitor his responses. Use your child's questions as a cue to tell you how much or how little he wants to know.

Honesty on the Job

As a person with panic disorder, chances are that if employed, you have missed work because of anxiety attacks. If you are like most panic sufferers, you have probably fabricated some convenient excuse such as a family emergency or being ill to justify your absences. But once the relief of diverting a panic attack faded, you most likely felt guilty and ashamed for being a liar. "Why couldn't I just tell them the truth?" you may have asked yourself. Are you, in fact, a deceitful employee that is too cowardly to be honest about a legitimate problem? Or, are you simply mindful that honesty comes with a price? You have enough anxiety already. The last thing you need to worry about is that you could lose your job because your employer might think that you are neurotic.

The decision to disclose an anxiety disorder to an employer is a dilemma that anxiety sufferers grapple with frequently. Clearly, there are advantages and disadvantages. To weigh these pros and cons of self-disclosure, you need to educate yourself about your legal rights in the workplace. The Americans With Disability Act of 1990 (ADA) was enacted to protect the rights of individuals with not only physical disabilities but psychiatric disabilities as well. It contains vital information about legislation regarding various aspects of self-disclosure, including:

- Confidentiality of records.
- Criterion for identifying a psychiatric disability.
- Which companies are mandated to adhere to the ADA and which are exempt.
- Implications for disclosing prior to or subsequent to being hired.
- Accommodations for disabilities.

Additionally, you can request a copy of a report from the Center of Mental Health Services of an ADA roundtable discussion. This discussion convened in January 1995 and was published in reader-friendly language. To order this document, consult the Resource section at the end of this book.

Disclosure of your panic disorder is a very personal decision. Unfortunately, research suggests that more people are uncomfortable with someone who has a psychiatric disability than a physical disability. Some employers associate the potential for violence in the workplace with hiring someone with a psychiatric disability. Stereotypes and ignorance run rampant, particularly in larger corporations where your relationship with co-workers and higher-ups may not be as intimate.

Nonetheless, the benefits of disclosing could entitle you to certain accommodations, providing it does not interfere with the performance of your job. Self-disclosure is a serious issue for consideration. You may wish to discuss your concerns with a family member, friend, or even your physician. Utilize the resources and support available through various health and human service organizations.

MASKING THE SYMPTOMS

Alcohol is the most widely abused substance today. Millions of Americans suffer from alcoholism. It is estimated that as many as twenty percent of those who drink have a panic disorder of which they are unaware. These people use alcohol to reduce their anxiety, which they may attribute to career stress, financial pressures, social inhibitions, marital problems, etc. As the alcohol begins to work and they sense their anxiety decreasing, these individuals come to rely more and more on its effects as a way to prevent panic attacks. A classic example of this process of self-medication is the case of Barry.

Case Study: Barry grew up in an alcoholic family. Beginning at age fifteen, he would have a few beers with his friends. Barry continued to drink socially throughout his college career, as alcohol use was encouraged at his fraternity house and at most social functions.

He graduated with an engineering degree. Four prominent aircraft manufacturers offered him positions, all at generous salaries. Barry was on top of the world. He could have his pick of the best jobs in his field. He had met a wonderful woman in school and planned to marry her once he started working. Everything was looking promising, but Barry's alcohol consumption increased. He thought he was merely unwinding when he drank, but in actuality, he was drinking because he continued to be anxious, particularly when he needed to drive long distances. At those times he would drink before he left the house and again after he arrived at his destination. If he had to fly somewhere, he would have four or five cocktails on the plane, depending on how long he was in the air.

When he was twenty-three, Barry was married. Sometime later, after his wife expressed concern over his drinking, he stopped for three weeks. During that time, he was irritable, had nightmares and insomnia, felt disoriented, and canceled appointments that were a distance from home. He also felt his heart beating very rapidly, even while resting. Every time he started to go into a store, he had to turn around and leave. He did not know why.

To gain some relief, Barry started drinking again, even more heavily than before, and his anxiety seemed to disappear. This continued until his wife threatened to leave him. It was at this point that he sought psychotherapy. It was clear to me that Barry was suffering from panic disorder, which he attempted to medicate by using alcohol. Barry quit drinking, joined Alcoholics Anonymous (AA), and was given a mild prescription for Ativan, with the understanding that he take it only if he had a panic attack too severe to manage on his own. Twice-weekly therapy provided Barry with the techniques necessary to confront and overcome his anxiety. After six months, he learned to trust his ability to manage his anxiety without the use of alcohol.

OVEREATING

Case Study: Beth has always enjoyed eating, but for the last several years she has been eating more frequently and has found that her thoughts always seem to revolve around food. She is a member of Overeaters Anonymous (OA) and has tried a number of weight loss programs. Still, she is always aware of wanting to eat, no matter how recently she has had her last meal.

Five years ago Beth had dental surgery. Her periodontist used novocaine with epinephrine to stop excessive bleeding. Epinephrine in some individuals can cause heart palpitations, perspiration, increased heart rate, and extreme anxiety. Beth became frightened and her dentist, aware that she had not eaten before surgery, suggested she immediately get something soft to eat to help combat the effects of the drug. Beth felt better after a large lunch, which included a special dessert as compensation for what she had gone through.

Subconsciously, Beth made the association between food and the dissipation of anxiety and, after her experience at the dentist's office, she developed the habit of compulsive eating. She was not conscious of her concern that another panic attack might occur—a typical reaction for anyone who experiences a panic episode. Beth, however, was using food almost like preventive medicine, believing unconsciously that as long as she kept herself from getting hungry, she would be spared from experiencing anxiety.

Each time Beth tried to delay eating, she would become restless. She was unaware that the restlessness was a prelude to anxiety. Before the anxiety could fully manifest, Beth indulged herself and the irritability would leave. She thus had two choices—to be overweight and anxiety-free or to be slim and irritable.

In discussing Beth's behavior, it is important to differentiate between anxiety and the physical symptoms of a hypoglycemic reaction to low blood sugar. Beth was not diagnosed as hypoglycemic. In addition, a hypoglycemic reaction usually occurs only when the person ingests too many carbohydrates and/or eats fewer than every four hours or so. Beth ate something at least once an hour.

Eventually, Beth came to realize that she was afraid of getting another panic attack. She found her way to my office. Once she was treated for panic disorder, her compulsive overeating changed. Beth now feels much better about herself. She continues to go to OA meetings as well as to practice the techniques that she learned in therapy to help her overcome her disorder.

ANOREXIA AND ANXIETY

Anorexia nervosa is an eating disorder. Over three percent of the college population suffers from this disease and most of its victims are white, middle- and upper-class teenage girls.

Many people believe that anorexia involves a loss of appetite, but in fact it is not a loss of appetite that causes its associated weight loss but a deliberate intention to withhold nutrition. The anorexic maintains a distorted body image and so she purposely refuses to eat, even when hungry.

The exact cause of anorexia is still vague. What is clear is that a profile of common characteristics exists for anorexics. For example, the most common ages of onset are the years between ages 14 and 18. Anorexics usually have parents who are commonly older and one parent who has always been an obsessive weight watcher. Most often, there is at least one other sibling in the family. The anorexic is often an overachiever who has very low self-esteem.

Anorexia and panic disorder appear superficially to have little in common. In fact, in certain respects anorexia can seem to be the polar opposite of panic disorder. For example, one of the key features of anorexia is the denial of one's mortality. One anorexic I know had to have a pacemaker implanted because of the damage her heart sustained from her disease.

Even after nearly dying, she was unable to eat enough food to maintain a healthy body weight.

This person is a very bright woman who fully understood that unless she ate, she would die. Unfortunately, the irrational belief that she was invincible continued to convince her that despite what she was told by her doctors, she could starve herself without facing the consequences. Consciously, this woman recognized that she was behaving irrationally, yet she could not stop herself from allowing that destructive inner voice to take over.

Conversely, a panic disorder sufferer is obsessed with her mortality. The irrational voice continues to haunt her with threats of danger where danger does not exist. What, then, do these vastly different diseases have in common? Anxiety and avoidance.

Anorexia is considered to be an avoidance behavior. In fact, once an anorexic has learned to avoid food successfully, she will often develop a phobia of it. Hence, she may recognize that eating is critical to her survival, but when she sits down to eat a meal, she feels anxious. The anxiety causes more avoidance and the phobia of food is reinforced. This is one reason why only twenty-five percent of anorexics will be able to recover completely. It is also one reason why Zanax, an antianxiety medication used to treat panic disorder, is used by anorexics to help them eat.

The similarities between anorexia and panic disorder by now should be fairly clear. Even more interesting is that many people with panic disorder have had a history of anorexia. According to some studies, thirty-eight percent of anorexics have had severe panic attacks and thirteen percent were agoraphobic. There are numerous factors for such a strong relationship between panic disorder and anorexia; the most significant of them are biological. Anorexics are deprived of essential nutrients because of their refusal to eat. The longstanding depletion of vitamins and minerals in their bodies begins to put a great deal of stress on the heart as well as on other organs. Potassium, sodium and other necessary electrolytes are lost and dehydration occurs. During dehydration, the already taxed heart has to pump even harder and this causes palpitations. In addition, the loss of vital nutrients results in dizziness, forgetfulness, mood swings and shaky limbs, as well as in an inability to concentrate. If a genetic predisposition toward panic disorder is present, the body in its weakened state is ripe for a panic attack.

ONGOING EMOTIONAL TRAUMA AND ANXIETY

Domestic Violence

Each year in the United States there are nearly three million reported cases of domestic violence. Domestic violence is responsible for more injuries to women between the ages of fifteen and forty-four than automobile accidents, rapes and muggings combined. Domestic violence is not restricted to any one group or community. Its grip penetrates all ethnic, social, economic, and even gender barriers. In fact, domestic violence is considered to be one of the largest health problems in the gay and lesbian community.

Earlier in this book, you read about posttraumatic stress disorder. Panic disorder causes unpredictable episodes of fear to erupt without apparent reason. The anxiety generated by PTSD can usually be linked to a specific situation that was particularly traumatic. The prefix of this disorder, "post," suggests that the incident has already occurred and that the disorder remains as a consequence of the emotional residue initiated by the event.

But what if the trauma is ongoing? If PTSD can cause such significant symptoms of anxiety and depression in someone many years subsequent to experiencing a trauma, can you imagine what can happen to an individual who is experiencing repeated trauma from which they cannot escape?

Living with the constant fear that harm will come to you and/or your children on a daily basis is absolutely terrifying. Moreover, in an attempt to live in such a frightful world, victims of domestic violence often remain in denial about the potential to be seriously injured or worse. Rather than getting help, they often tell themselves that the situation will improve. This, in turn, creates more anxiety because deluding yourself into a false sense of safety is only putting you at greater risk. Unconsciously, the victim is aware of this and so she lives in a constant state of conflict and fear. If you review the warning signs of domestic abuse on Table 2.1 and identify with at least two or more of the items listed, you may be living with domestic violence. If this is the case, please call the hotline numbers listed in the Resource section and 911 emergency to access immediate help. Do not allow yourself to believe that you are responsible for the violent episodes of your partner. It is not your fault and your anxiety is trying to tell you something.

Panic Attack

You are standing on a railroad crossing and suddenly you observe a train approaching you at speeds exceeding sixty miles an hour. As you move to get out of the path of the train, you notice that your shoe is caught on a portion of the track. Try as you may, you cannot extricate yourself. You look up and see that the powerful locomotive is now only seconds away from crushing you. You know you are about to die and there is nothing that can save you. Your heart pounds furiously, your entire body trembles uncontrollably as you fall to your knees and with a prayer on your lips, whisper "please don't let me die." Braced for your demise, you notice the piercing screech of the train's brakes. A split second later and it would have been too late but, by some miracle, you were spared a horrifying death.

Onlookers rush to you and offer comfort and assistance. You are driven to the nearest hospital for medical evaluation. The physician on call recommends a psychotherapist to help you cope with such a traumatic ordeal. During your initial appointment, the therapist asks detailed questions about your sleeping cycle, nightmares, anxiety, depression, etc. She tells you that probably if not now but in the near future, you will suffer symptoms associated with posttraumatic stress disorder and recommends that you stay in therapy for a long time to help you resolve

Table 2.1 ━━━━━━━━━━━━━━━━━━━━━━━━━━━━━━━━

ABUSIVE BEHAVIORS

Physical
- Hitting
- Choking
- Pushing
- Restraining
- Punching
- Using objects to hit
- Forcing sex or sexual behaviors that the victim is uncomfortable performing.

Intimidation
- Using language that suggests threats of harm to you, your children, or your pets
- Using weapons to threaten injury or death
- Destroying property
- Throwing things
- Punching walls.

Verbal Abuse
- Shouting
- Name calling
- Using degrading language

Isolation
- Taking economic control
- Monitoring telephone calls and mail
- Insisting that you spend less time with family and friends
- Saying things to your family and friends to alienate them from you
- Overly jealous and accusing you of being unfaithful
- Violating your work place by going to your job or constantly calling you there, despite requests to leave you alone.

your difficulties. Family members, friends, perhaps even the media rally around you in support. You feel relief that as horrible as it was, it is over. And with the love and encouragement of those close to you, you feel optimistic that you will be in tip-top shape very soon.

But the next day, the same incident occurs again, only on a different set of train tracks. And once again, you narrowly escape facing death by a heartbeat. Several hours later that same day, it occurs again, only in another part of town. And soon you find that on a daily basis, despite every precaution you take to avoid an oncoming train, it seems to appear out of nowhere, and you are always just moments away from annihilation. Moreover, no one seems to be rallying around you in support. In fact, when you share your story of near death, your experiences are for the most part minimized. You find yourself existing in a nightmare of unremitting trauma, day after day, not knowing when or if it will ever cease. What do you imagine happens to an organism exposed to repeated trauma? The *impact* of the trauma increases with frequency. So, we remove the train from the scenario, and what changes? Unfortunately, not much. Each time you have a panic attack, particularly if you believe that you are dying, you are traumatized. You may or may not experience nightmares and/or depression along with your anxiety as you might if you received a formal diagnosis of posttraumatic stress disorder. Nonetheless, you are for all intents and purposes suffering from a very similar disorder, only your trauma, like domestic violence, is ongoing.

Understanding the breadth of your symptoms is critical to your recovery. So what's next, you may ask? Remember in our analogy of the oncoming train, there was a supportive therapist ready to help you overcome your symptoms of PTSD? If she was familiar with the latest treatments for PTSD, she might have utilized something called "Imaginal Exposure Therapy." There are various approaches to treating trauma, but this one has enjoyed a long history of success for trauma survivors. Imaginal Exposure Therapy is a very potent intervention and should only be implemented by a competent therapist familiar with its utilization. The therapy involves assisting the client in retrieving the memories of a traumatic episode and carefully guiding him through reliving it in a safe and supportive environment.   In this way, the individual is given the opportunity to express all the emotions that may have been quelled by the shock associated with the actual experience. Often clients will cry, get angry and feel a sense of loss. Occasionally, the body has its own reactions. In extreme cases, even urination or defecation occur. But slowly the client is able to accept that the trauma is over. The psychic overload generated by the traumatic event is diffused and the attending anxiety and depression soon abates.

Imaginal Exposure Therapy is not appropriate for you to attempt on your own. However, you can utilize a safe, modified adaptation to assist you in changing your relationship with your past and present associations with panic.   You can do this through the use of an exercise I call "**Controlled Regression**." Controlled Regression is a method that is safe to do alone. The following steps will show you how.

1.   Familiarize yourself with the section on Meditation in Chapter 6.

2.   While in a relaxed state, recall your first panic attack. Notice how your body started to feel different. Remember as vividly as possible where you were and how you experienced the anxiety to escalate. You may notice as you do this exercise that your body actually develops some of the same anxiety symptoms. Do not let this frighten you. This is supposed to happen. You may open your eyes at any time to stop the experience. However, you should bear in mind that the goal here is to allow you to access the unpleasant memory of your previous panic episodes so that you can release the historic hold it has on you.

As you proceed with the memory of your first panic attack, practice the traditional deep breathing exercises delineated in Chapter 3. At this point, you may continue to experience fear or other emotions associated with feeling helpless. Let the feelings be expressed and released with each cleansing exhale. Acknowledge the depth of pain, but remind yourself that it already occurred and is now over. This means your past no longer has power over you. Go a step further and rewrite your emotional history. See the same incident occurring again, but this time, in your relaxed state, imagine yourself taking control by refusing to allow the anxiety to debilitate you. Observe yourself feeling empowered instead of paralyzed. Make certain to imagine yourself smiling and feeling in control. Then open your eyes, and take another deep breath. You may notice an immediate affect or it may take some time. The exercise is not completed, however, until you eventually go back to each and every situation you can remember when you had panicked. Follow the very same steps and continue to do this for each panic attack past and present. Each time you release the fear and remind yourself that the past need not dictate your future, you are that much closer to ending the pattern of habituation that occurs with repeated trauma.

AGORAPHOBIA IN MODERN SOCIETY

Agoraphobia is literally Greek for "fear of the marketplace." From its name, you can appreciate that such fear is as old as civilization. And yet, somehow, it seems to make little sense. Can you imagine, for example, that two hundred years ago, a strong, healthy young man might be frightened of traveling from his village down the road to the central marketplace? It can be difficult to conceive of anyone getting panic attacks during the preindustrial era; most objects of fear are post-industrial: airplanes, elevators, large supermarkets, cars on trips far away from home, etc. One would not expect anxiety to occur in such simple surroundings.

But what if you are a woman? It would appear that there is nothing particularly threatening about sitting in a coach and buggy traveling to the general store if you are a man. But women traveling alone have always had reason to be concerned for their safety. No one would think twice if a young lady asked a gentleman to accompany her to the marketplace. Reverse the players and the request would seem very odd. Can you picture the kind of ridicule a young man might endure if he were to admit that he was frightened of going across town on his own? As you might imagine, he would probably become the laughingstock of his community.

Now transport the same man into the future, let us say into Los Angeles, California in April 1992. Out of his window, he sees a black wall of smoke rising slowly above the market that had just burned during a riot the previous night. The sound of fire engines and newscasters fill his head as he tries to decide whether or not to drive to work that morning. This man is an attorney employed at a law firm in downtown Los Angeles. Deciding that he cannot put off the inevitable, he embarks across town. His favorite scenic route has been reduced to ashes and smoke. Onlookers kneel before their fire-eaten businesses, sobbing in disbelief and horror. What this gentleman once recognized as landmarks on his journey into town have been nearly destroyed.

After a rather unproductive day at the office, our young man, reaching for his keys, notices that he feels a little funny. As he approaches his car, he experiences a shaky, light-headed sensation in his body. He starts his car and notices that driving seems to have taken on a whole new dimension. Our young attorney is now scanning the streets very carefully while driving. He quickly locks both doors and calls a friend from his car phone in order to distract himself from his anxiety. Once he arrives home, he feels relieved. That night on the news, however, he learns about some young women in a shopping mall who were gunned down in cold blood for their car. Following this, at least once a week, our attorney listens to reports of carjackings or innocent children being murdered in the line of gang gunfire. This man has a best friend who was shot at his bank's ATM during a robbery in broad daylight for only sixty dollars. And if this weren't enough, rumors continue to circulate that the gangs have formed an allegiance with one another for the sheer purpose of annihilating the city. This individual would be foolish if he did not sequester himself in his home until the danger had passed. In other words, being homebound is an appropriate behavior if leaving home is threatening. Clearly, the L. A. riots were a threatening situation. However, it doesn't stop there. Crime is on the rise. Gangs are no longer limited to tiny factions of the inner cities. In addition, the invention of auto alarms has created a new type of crime wave—carjackings. Although certain types of cars are at greater risk of being carjacked, there still is no guarantee it won't happen to you or someone you know. Gang warfare, ATM robberies, carjackings, freeway shootings, riots; welcome to the modern society! Why emphasize all these life-threatening situations? Because the reality is that there are times when your agoraphobia may not be an "irrational fear." It is nearly impossible to ignore the current state of the world, particularly if you live in a metropolitan area.

Perhaps you think that by clearly delineating all of the reasons why you should not leave your home, there is cause for you to remain agoraphobic. I think not. I certainly hope that you will recognize how difficult it may be to function nowadays without concern for your well being; at the same time, such concern must not paralyze you. Although it is true that some unfortunate individuals may be the victims of violent crime, there is no reason to believe that you will be singled out. In addition, there are certain measures you can take to minimize the risk of harm to yourself. You can be aware of your environment, keep your car doors locked at all times, do your banking indoors, and develop a list of rules by which you feel safer in the world. Existence itself exposes us to all kinds of risks. If you try to avoid all risks, you will avoid living. Move forward, take precautions; try not to confuse fear with circumspection.

Chapter 3

CAN I BE CURED?

YOU ARE NOT YOUR DISEASE

I recall a morning that made its indelible mark on my psyche.

It was a morning that had been preceded by one of the most romantic evenings I'd ever had. I awakened next to the person I believed would be my partner for life. His tender kiss was my cue to open my eyes. As he rolled over and embraced me, I could feel myself falling even more deeply in love with him. He must have sensed the intensity of my emotions and drew me even closer to his body, holding me firmly against his chest. I lay with him, enraptured. All seemed right with the world.

Suddenly, I realized I wasn't getting enough air—or so I thought. As I pulled away, his grasp only grew tighter. I began to notice that I was feeling anxious. My partner's arms, which were heretofore a loving sanctuary from the fearsome real world, transformed themselves into what felt like a broken elevator on the thirtieth floor of a skyscraper. I was no longer a little anxious, I was beginning to panic. "LET ME GO!" I shouted.

"Gee, what did you think I was going to do?"

"I don't know," I replied. "I felt completely out of control when I could not get up." Then I heard it. The one word

71

I have heard ever since I had my first panic attack. The one word that always made me feel humiliated.

"You're really idiosyncratic, aren't you?"

I could hardly blame him. After all, the poor guy put up with a lot. I thought of all those times in the car when it was not moving and the windows were rolled up all the way and I demanded we either move or roll the windows down, and preferably do both. No one has fully understood the behavior I acted out on a daily basis.

Throughout my years as a panic disorder sufferer, each close friend or lover has accused me of being strange. Eventually I came to believe that being peculiar is, in fact, part of my identity. I have been fortunate enough to have many people care about me. Still, there are two common characteristics assigned to me that have echoed through each relationship I have ever had. People have found me controlling and difficult (indeed, on occasion, a "nightmare" to be with). I have learned that, although I have plenty of other attributes and I have never been at a loss for friends or lovers, I have challenged these people. Consequently, I have been surprised that they have continued to genuinely care about me. But how could someone be such "a nightmare" to deal with and still be lovable? My self-image had been formed by the unique way in which others perceived me. I had a particular identity. But it was an identity that carried with it great feelings of inadequacy, no matter how much love and affection I was given. I often lived in horror that, once I was discovered, once my aberrant behavior reared its ugly head, my partners in love or life would desert me.

Of course, this has not been the case. In fact, the reverse has been true. Even those friends who were privy to my eccentricities still care about me. This is because I am more than the sum total of my symptoms of panic disorder, as is any sufferer of this disease. But you should note that this kind of struggle for acceptance often accompanies panic disorder. For this reason, it is important to examine not only how identity develops in someone with this disease, but all of the ramifications of the particular identify formed. To fully understand this process, it will be necessary to separate the symptoms of your disease from your core personality.

Let us take a closer look at identity formation in the panic disorder sufferer by using your own experiences. Think back to a time before your first panic attack. This may be difficult if you have had panic disorder for a long time or as a child. If this is the case, it probably seems as if you have always been a little different from your peers. Perhaps you were afraid to engage in sports, to be away from home, to go on trail rides, climb trees, etc. You may have perceived the world as a dangerous place, not only for you but for others, too. Of course, male children exhibiting idiosyncratic or fearful behavior will usually be subjected to more ridicule and alienation than female children. Still, it is very difficult for both male and female children to endure the stares and whispers of disapproval. One could grow up with pervasive feelings that she/he couldn't measure up. This may be your situation.

If you did not grow up feeling anxious, it will be valuable for you to make a list of all of the personality characteristics attributed to you before the onset of your first panic attack. For example, you may recall having been told as a child that you were "patient." Include that quality in your *"before"* list. Continue to identify positive qualities in yourself. When the *before* list is complete, make a column next to it listing the traits that you and others have found to be negative qualities as a panic disorder sufferer. List those side by side. Your two lists may look something like this:

Before Anxiety Characteristics:	After Anxiety Characteristics:
Flexible	Controlling
Patient	Impatient
Rebellious/adventurous	Fearful
Healthy	Body looks/feels sick
Outgoing	Reclusive
Accommodating	Manipulative/demanding

Before Anxiety Characteristics:	After Anxiety Characteristics:
Spontaneous	Tolerates no surprises (needs to be prepared at all times)
Passionate	Obsessive

These would appear to describe two entirely different people. One person is someone you yourself may want to get to know. The other may seem to be someone you may not want as a friend. Which one are you? You are the person on the left; your disease is the person on the right. Panic disorder causes symptoms. Symptoms, in turn, determine behavior. Behaviors become confused with personality. Your friends and family should be aware that they have two relationships; one with you and another with your disease.

If you are someone who had this disease beginning in childhood, your basic personality traits may be a little more difficult to assess. But, as before, you can start by creating two columns:

Activities that I Liked	Things of which I was Afraid
Studying the stars	An observatory
Wading in the ocean	Swimming
Staying overnight with my cousins	Spending the night away from home
Going to plays and wanting to act	Performing
Communing with nature	Climbing mountains and trees
The adventure of travel	Going on overnight trips
Raising animals and exercising	Horseback riding

Of course, your list may not be quite so symmetrical but you can see the relationship between fear and avoidance. The fear associated with each activity is responsible for causing the limitations. It is the limitations that may be perceived by both the child and the child's peers as peculiar. The child then grows up consistently believing that she/he is hard to deal with. The same identity formation can apply to you even if you have had your onset of panic later in life. It makes no difference when your fears developed. Either way, idiosyncratic behavior can create all kinds of emotions that usually include a strong fear of abandonment. Many panic disorder sufferers feel so unworthy that they cannot relinquish the fear that their spouse or lover will leave them. One example of this problem of negative identity formation can be illustrated in the following case history.

Case Study: Rick was referred to my office because of panic attacks that he suffered after learning that he had tested positive for the HIV virus. He was 26, handsome and bright. During the consultation, I learned that, although the diagnosis had put Rick into crisis, he already had a long and intimate relationship with anxiety. He had been agoraphobic for nearly ten years. As his treatment progressed, he slowly began to accept the magnitude of his HIV status. His concerns about becoming ill became much stronger. Rick had only a handful of friends, most of whom were not very close. One day, he broke down and wept as he shared his belief that his being agoraphobic meant that he was unlovable.

It is not uncommon for some people to be afraid to cultivate a relationship, romantic or otherwise, with someone who is HIV-positive. Sometimes, friendships, romantic relationships, even familial relationships are dissolved out of an erroneous fear that the disease will spread to others. In addition, many people are afraid of becoming emotionally involved with someone who may soon become ill and die. Interestingly, those were not Rick's primary concerns. Rick's issues focused on his agoraphobia and on how others might react to it.

Rick believed for many years that he was too hard to love. He experienced a significant amount of self-hatred. Rick identified strongly with his disease. Much of the work we did in therapy was designed to help him discern the behaviors dictated by his agoraphobia—his co-personality. With treatment, Rick's anxiety symptoms began to abate until he was able to become acquainted with a new identity. Once Rick's real identity was fully recognized, he began to feel confident in establishing and maintaining relationships. He was able to accept that one day his HIV virus might cause him to become ill—that he might need to break commitments just as he had done so many times when he was particularly anxious and couldn't leave the house. The difference was that Rick was now able to understand that canceling plans did not necessarily make him unreliable. Cancellations are an appropriate course of action under certain circumstances.

Rick's recovery, not only from his anxiety but from his negative self perception, may have an application to your situation. If you have canceled plans, been afraid to make commitments, and have lived by a multitude of rules and regulations regarding what you will and will not do, you have been acting out behaviors dictated by your anxiety. You are not a bad person. Unless you understand this, your recovery will be impaired. Try to have compassion for all you have had to endure.

TAKE A DEEP BREATH

Breathing Exercises

Imagine yourself in a lush garden, inhaling the fragrances of orange blossoms, honeysuckle, and jasmine. Picture yourself lying down on cool green grass with a light breeze gently blowing your hair as the sun delicately caresses your skin. Allow this image to linger for a few minutes with your eyes closed and while you're in a reclining position. You may notice that the images themselves seem to lull you into a tranquil state of mind. Now place your hands over your abdomen and notice how easy your breath moves through you. Without your conscious awareness, your body has most likely made a shift in your breathing rate. Simultaneously you may notice a reduction in your anxiety.

Continue lying in the same position. Rather than visualizing a garden, see yourself in an elevator with the door about to close. Notice anything? If you place your hand on your chest and abdomen, you may notice a significant difference in your breathing pattern. Perhaps you will find that, in fact, your chest and stomach seem to be almost completely still. Whereas the garden image automatically allowed deeper breathing, the elevator image instantaneously creates an inhibition of breathing. There is a term for this relationship. It is called "autogenic." It is based upon the principle that the mind and body are one; if the mind is disturbed, the body will naturally follow. Autogenic training is often used in conjunction with biofeedback to teach the patient how to put him or herself into a comfortable state of mind. Fortunately, doing so does not require a biofeedback machine.

The following are specific breathing techniques you can practice on your own. These exercises are very important because the panic disorder sufferer often underbreathes while in a resting state. Breathing is frequently shallow. If your breathing is shallow while in a calm state, you can imagine what happens when you are confronted with an anxiety-producing situation. Often, shallow breathing can turn into hyperventilation, a state that is caused from holding onto too much oxygen. When you breathe in oxygen, you are supposed to release it a second or two later. The oxygen converts to carbon dioxide in your body. That is what you actually inhale. Hyperventilation occurs when there is no conversion because you are not releasing the oxygen. The results of hyperventilation are not dangerous, so you certainly do not need to alarm yourself. They are, however, uncomfortable, producing many of the symptoms of a panic episode. Shaky legs, heart racing, tingling in arms and extremities, difficulty speaking or understanding others—these are all symptoms of hyperventilation, which is often interpreted as a panic attack. One immediate intervention to be used when this occurs is to breathe into a paper bag. The paper bag will lock in the carbon dioxide and help to regulate normal breathing. But the best intervention is prevention.

Read on carefully. If you try a technique that causes you to feel a little lightheaded, note that it may be due to an increase of oxygen to which you are unaccustomed. If the dizziness causes you to feel anxious, stop the exercise and modify it so that you can feel more comfortable.

Traditional Slow Breathing Exercise

This method is probably used more frequently for feelings of stress and discomfort. It is easy to use and may feel as if it is a little more in sync with the way you normally breathe. This is one reason why you may wish to try this first and observe its results before attempting the rapid release exercise. This exercise is also used for swimming, singing and other activities requiring an even distribution of air flow. If you enjoy either of these activities, you may want to imagine yourself engaging in one of these as you practice this breathing technique. Visualization and breathing can best be utilized in concert with one another. If you do not care for either activity, try to picture yourself in a safe environment as you pay close attention to how you are doing the exercise.

For our purposes, let us say that you enjoy swimming. Try to see yourself getting into a calm, crisp pool on a glorious sunny afternoon. The water may at first be a bit chilly and your instincts will tell you to take one long breath before you go under water. Listen to your inclinations. Imagine that, as you draw your breath through your nose, it comes from a different place—from your *abdomen,* not your chest. Take a moment to feel your abdominal muscles with your hands. Place your hands just below your rib cage and note that as you draw your air from below your lungs, your abdominal muscles move up and down. Your hand should be rising and falling with each breath. Now release the breath by exhaling slowly out of your mouth.

As you become acquainted with this feeling, see yourself submerged in a shallow lap pool—one just large enough to accommodate you without seeming overwhelming. Imagine entering the water and taking seven or eight strokes before coming up for air. This may seem difficult at first, so you may need to pace yourself. You can finally let your head up on the seventh stroke, releasing the air evenly and you will have mastered this technique.

As mentioned earlier, swimming is only one of several ways in which to practice visualization and breathing. The reason why it is important to attach an image to this exercise is two-fold.

First, you should get into the habit of distraction. When a panic attack occurs, your mind repeats excessive and irrational thoughts. Your thought patterns form quickly and can hurl through your mind and body with great speed. What can occur next is a feeling of being trapped. One can say you have entered into an emotional gridlock. You can liken this to being caught in a traffic jam on the freeway. You would then have two options—to panic or to relax. Panicking would not be too hard to do. Relaxing is the difficult part.

You have probably tried repeated times to relax on your own and found that it does not seem to work at the critical moment. This is because relaxation and desperation are incompatible. The more desperate one is to relax, the more that relaxation will elude them. Relaxation by its very definition means to let go and surrender. As long as you are pushing to surrender, it will not happen. What is likely to occur instead is an intensification of your feelings of desperation, which translate into more anxiety. Using distraction is one way you can manage emotional gridlock. Learning to develop an internalized mechanism that acts to police emotional gridlock, you can then guide your thoughts into becoming more peripheral than central.

Just as the highway patrol enters into a traffic jam and clears a path for travel, you can do the same. The automobiles may still be on the road, but they are directed to a place that allows your vehicle the freedom to move forward. Your willingness to participate in life is your vehicle. Until now, your response to anxiety was to automatically panic, but now you can learn a new response, beginning with distraction. If images of swimming do not appeal to you, use other images that do.

Create an image that will illustrate a way to hold the breath coming from your abdomen and allow you to release it in about eight seconds.

The second reason why visualization of swimming can be helpful is that water is often a symbol to the unconscious of safety and relaxation. We did, after all, spend nine months in the womb, floating in symbiotic fluid. If swimming causes some anxiety, all the better! Using images of swimming while breathing (as instructed) may help to change your associations and make it easier to be around a pool or ocean in the future. Either way, I recommend it!

Rapid Release Breathing Exercise

This technique is very effective not only for stress but for pain relief and anxiety reduction as well. The exercise may seem a little strange because it is a more aggressive breathing technique; but it can yield dramatic results. In order to utilize this technique effectively, it would be helpful to prepare yourself for a shift in your awareness. What I mean by "awareness" is the spectrum of sensations you experience. These sensations may include a range of emotions, often beginning with a feeling of exultation or excitement and mellowing to a feeling of release, sometimes even sadness. Often feelings of sadness can be easily masked when breathing is shallow. Although anxiety may be a biological reaction to which panic disorder sufferers are predisposed, there remains an emotional component which must not be overlooked. When an individual is anxious, she/he exists in a state of hypervigilance and self-obsessive thoughts. Emotions can get lost in scenarios of danger and threat. For this reason, many valid feelings and reactions to living become consumed by fear. When this happens and the fear is released, the emotions themselves may emerge. Deep breathing can provide a way for the anxiety to exit the body, creating a space in which to experience feelings. The steps to this are easy.

1.   Inhale through your nose, nine short breaths; hold for one second and exhale slowly out of your mouth.

2.   Repeat this exercise at least five times.   Then rest

a few minutes. Resume again and stop. You may continue again or as often as needed. Once you have mastered the various deep breathing techniques outlined, you are ready to move to the next step, called progressive relaxation.

PROGRESSIVE RELAXATION: STRESS VS ANXIETY

Progressive relaxation is a term used to describe the process by which you can induce yourself into deep relaxation.

When you think of someone who is under a lot of stress, what comes to mind? If you examine the phrase, "under a lot of stress", it implies that stress is some outside force weighing heavily upon the victim. This is because, for the most part, it is a fairly accurate description, albeit a melodramatic one. Stress is external; anxiety is internal. We do not say that someone is under a lot of anxiety; we use words like "experiencing, having, feeling." Anxiety may cause stressful reactions which usually arise from an internal belief or misperception. The following case history illustrates this distinction quite well.

Case Study: Mary is 32 years old and married to a very successful attorney. Mary has excellent health, a wonderful relationship with her husband and a great deal of free time because she is not employed. Mary has very little stress in her life, yet she is always anxious. She will tell you that the source of her anxiety is the market, or airplanes, or the constant pain in her back that no doctor can diagnose accurately. Mary is convinced she has cancer, despite results from a battery of tests that clearly rule out any malignancies. Mary is anxious because she equates pain with disease and death. She also tells herself that she will have a panic attack every time she goes into a market and, as you might guess, she does in fact have one. The source of her anxiety is not the market or her body pains, rather, it is what they represent and how she interprets that information that is the source of her anxiety. Markets equal danger. Body pains represent death. Anxiety, in and of itself, is produced from the inside out. Stress is produced from the outside in. A new job, divorce, traffic jams, work-related deadlines, are all situations which may cause stress related symptoms. But these should not be confused with anxiety. Feeling agitated because you were late and stuck in traffic is different than getting a panic attack the moment the local market's doors open. Anxiety is based upon irrational fears; stress is often a reaction to rational and reasonable circumstances.

A clear understanding of the difference between stress and anxiety are useful when trying to determine the most effective relaxation techniques to use for your own symptoms. Inappropriate techniques can sometimes worsen your symptoms. This is why, when embarking on exercises designed to relax you, you should be discriminating. For example, isometric exercises are frequently prescribed as a method for relaxation. Isometric exercises involve the conscious contraction and relaxation of certain muscle groups. In normal persons, these techniques allow each body part to expel tension, inducing a pleasant state of mind. But in many panic disorder sufferers, isometric exercises can increase anxiety. The reason is that they call attention to the body's imperfections. In some individuals, they cause them to believe that their muscles are overly contracted. This is because the panic disorder sufferer is typically relatively tense, even when in a relaxed state. Hence, too much attention paid to the body by the panic disorder sufferer may promote more fear.

Progressive Relaxation Exercise

You have already been familiarized with deep breathing and visualization. Progressive relaxation means combining visualization and breathing in order to create a calm and peaceful state of mind. You can begin by closing your eyes and then focusing your awareness on your feet. Imagine that a brilliant white or yellow light is located at the heels of your feet, just like a miniature sun. The light is warm and familiar. As you allow the light to warm your feet, visualize it moving upward from your feet into your ankles. Notice that the light seems to melt away unwanted feelings and sensations. See it slowly travel upward from the calves of your legs and then climb your entire body, limb by limb. Allow the light to bathe your body in a soft gentle glow. As you feel the warm sensation permeate your body, you will find that you become progressively more relaxed. You will find that the more relaxed your body is, the better you seem to feel. Enjoy the feeling that progressive relaxation provides. You're ready to take the next step.to combine visualization techniques with progressive relaxation techniques.

HEARING VOICES?

As you enter the market, you notice a little voice inside your head. The voice is yours, yet it seems removed from reality. It warns you that, if you enter the market, you will be severely punished. This voice sounds so convincing that you find yourself hesitating before the market doors. One step forward; two steps back. The voice booms in your head, "Don't go inside, you'll get a panic attack!" What do you do? If you are like most panic disorder sufferers, you will pay heed and retreat.

Inner dialogue is a constant process that humans use to think efficiently. These internal voices give shape to our ideas, feelings and fears. The decisions we make require us to pay close attention to these voices. Unfortunately, sometimes these voices can become your worst enemy. You may recall a discussion in an earlier chapter of how obsessive avoidant thoughts can be. This is the nature of the beast. The more fear one has, the more she/he will hear these voices becoming threatening. The following pages illustrate the panic cycle, and show how negative self-statements maintain and even exaggerate the symptoms of panic disorder.

If you examine the cycle closely, you will notice that the cycle begins and ends with panic. The beginning of the cycle is formed by expectations which are, in essence, negative self-statements.

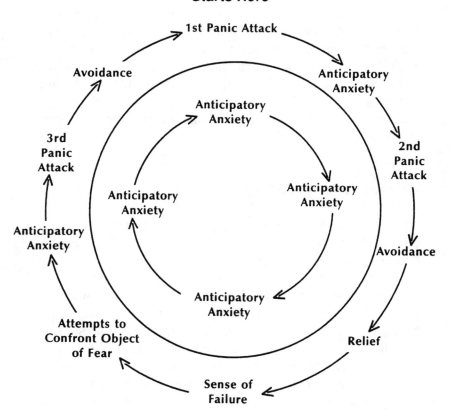

PANIC CYCLE
Starts Here

The following is a list of many of the thoughts panic disorder sufferers tell themselves.

Negative Self-Statements
1. I can't, I'll get a panic attack.
2. What if I get a panic attack?
3. I could never go there, I would be too anxious.
4. I'd better cancel, I can tell I'll be anxious.
5. If it's only 9:00 a.m. and I'm already this anxious, I will be like this all day.

6. If I don't leave now, I will lose my mind.
7. My heart is racing, I'm going to die.
8. I'm going crazy.
9. I can't be alone or I'll get a panic attack.
10. Once I get inside the elevator, it will close and I'll get stuck and I'll be trapped!
11. I can't breathe, I'm going to die!

Beliefs like this can immobilize you. How can you possibly have those types of thoughts and be willing to confront the source of your anxiety? As illustrated on the chart, these expectations keep your disease alive. Unless you can modify or change these inner recordings, the panic cycle will continue to run your life.

Transforming negative messages into positive ones is what is called the "cognitive behavioral" approach. The following chart will teach you how to IST: *IDENTIFY, STOP* and *TRANSFORM* your thoughts. IST is a formula you can use on yourself as an intervention technique the next time you feel anxious. Examine the IST chart carefully, then make your own chart that includes your most common thought patterns. After reviewing the IST chart, you should be able to apply the substance of the chart to almost any situation that elicits anxiety.

IST should become a routine part of your recovery. Perhaps you have already attempted to talk yourself out of feeling afraid

I	S	T
1. I can't, I'll get a panic attack.	Stop	I can do this even if I get anxious.
2. What if I get a panic attack?	Stop	I refuse to get a panic attack.
3. I could never go there, I would be too anxious.	Stop	I can drive there, even if I'm a little anxious.

I	S	T
4. I'd better cancel, I can tell I'll be too anxious.	Stop	I am going to go, I can handle it even if I get a little anxious.
5. It's only 9:00 a.m. and I'm already anxious, I will be like this all day.	Stop	Just because I feel poorly now, doesn't mean I'll feel bad all day.
6. If I don't leave now, I will lose my mind.	Stop	I *can* handle this, I'm not going crazy even though it feels that way.
7. My heart is racing, I'm going to die.	Stop	I am so anxious, my heart is beating more rapidly. I'm perfectly healthy, so it'll slow down in a few minutes.
8. I'm going crazy.	Stop	I *can* handle this, I'm not going to go crazy, even though it feels that way.
9. I can't be alone or I'll get a panic attack.	Stop	I'm perfectly safe alone, I can rely on myself to take care of myself.
10. Once I get inside the elevator, it will close and I'll get stuck and I'll be trapped!	Stop	The elevator won't get stuck, and even if it does, I'm perfectly safe and can call for help.
11. I can't breathe, I'm going to die!	Stop	When I'm anxious, my chest tightens a little and it makes it feel like I can't get enough air but, in fact, I'm getting all the air that I need.

and found that you were unable to do it. Do not feel discouraged. Practicing IST exclusively is difficult to master. It is best utilized in conjunction with other cognitive behavioral techniques. As you read on, you will learn that there are many tools available to you. Another cognitive behavioral technique you can try is distancing yourself from the anxiety. I call this, being a DETACHED OBSERVER.

The Detached Observer
There are two ways to watch a movie. You can view it as a spectator or become an emotional participant. Most people alternate back and forth, depending upon their mood, the content of the movie and those whose company they share. In most cases, the decision whether to participate in the movie or to merely observe it is an unconscious one; but, it does not have to be. Let us say, for example, that you are entertaining some friends. As you are viewing a movie that has been rented, some of the scenes evoke sadness. You may find yourself starting to cry. Just as your eyes begin to well up with tears, you might choose to distance yourself just a bit from the emotional content. Your concerns about an emotional display may cause you to put conscious controls on your subjective experience. This means that you are changing your experience from one of subjectivity to objectivity simply by choosing to do so. Believe it or not, you have the power to institute these controls over your own anxiety. In other words, the next time you feel anxious imagine that you are leaving your body and viewing the situation as an "observer." Watch yourself becoming anxious. Then rate your anxiety on a scale of 1 to 10, 10 being the absolute worst case. When you master these techniques, you will automatically become the spectator instead of the emotional participant. This technique is very valuable. What is more, you can use it to measure your success with this program. Try it the next time you are anxious. Then try it again after you have finished reading this book. The techniques that you will be learning should significantly reduce your anxiety. Your new rating system will afford you the opportunity to mark your own progress!

ANIMATED IMAGES

If you are a panic disorder sufferer, you may often feel as if your fear attacks you like a ferocious beast without notice or provocation. This beast seems to thrive on power. Each time you let the beast prevent you from attaining your goals the beast has won and you have lost.

In an attempt to demystify this beast, I have developed a technique that I call "animation visualization." This involves getting into a relaxed state, eyes closed. Then choose some character that looks ominous, e.g. Godzilla, and make this character into a cartoon. This cartoon represents your anxiety. Of course, you can choose a character that is already a cartoon. For example, a few of my clients have chosen "The Tasmanian Devil," a cartoon character that moves very quickly and causes much damage wherever it goes. There are various scenarios that can be created using animation visualization. The one I use most often is called "anger as power."

ANGER AS POWER

Anxiety is an invisible handicap, yet its impact can be as crippling as any neurological or muscular disorder. People who once led perfectly normal lives may become prisoners of their own minds. When you have anxiety, the person you once were seems to have died. Some agoraphobics cannot even venture outside long enough to check their own mail. What is interesting is that, in all the cases I have handled in which anxiety has been a longstanding problem, the client has rarely expressed anger at the dramatic difference in her/his lifestyle and relationships as a result of this anxiety. Such a client often expresses only fear and depression, and sometimes the wish to die. Such clients are defeated individuals who have given up because they do not know what else to do. They succumb silently to their own slow death, feeling a growing sense of helplessness every day. The following exercise can help.

While in a relaxed state, use animation visualization to initiate a dialogue with the monster (anxiety), stating the many ways in which it has limited your life. Tell it how your friendships, jobs or marriage have suffered. Continue listing the ways in which this monster has caused suffering. Then get angry and direct that anger at the monster. Interestingly, more often than not, many people require gentle coercing in order to feel angry. Their anger, I believe, is so enormous that it has been safely disguised by fear. Becoming aware of its magnitude can be very threatening. Consequently, both the "animation visualization" and the "anger as power" techniques provide a safe place for the anger to be acknowledged and discharged.

As your dialogues with the beast continue, your anger will begin to feel more genuine. Sometimes it is helpful to speak the dialogue out loud rather than conduct it silently. Hearing your voice and words forces you to stay in touch with your anger.

After you have acknowledged your anger and directed it accordingly, there are numerous scenarios that can be used.

Fight, Not Flight

Imagine a boxing ring. See yourself in one corner with boxing gloves on. In the other corner is the cartoon monster with his boxing shorts on. Before the bell sounds, you and the monster touch each other's glove in a gesture of friendship. Try to look directly into the monster's eyes. As you stare into the eyes of your enemy, notice an expression of sadness and vulnerability. For the first time, this monster looks as though he, too, is scared.

The bell sounds, and the two of you meet in the center of the ring. First, observe your opponent. He will use every tactic to trick you into thinking that he is more powerful than he really is. He may suddenly expand, or change appearance, or make ugly sounds. In reality, he is harmless and, although he may be trying to frighten you, he cannot succeed. As the beast moves closer, do not move. As he throws punches, visualize yourself blocking them. Continue this until your opponent grows weary.

At this point, see yourself moving forward and decking the monster with a solid punch. The referee counts from one to ten, and before he finishes counting, the monster will be getting up, ready to hit again. As he approaches, weak and shaky, hit him one more time, knocking him out. This time you have won. Visualize the referee raising your arm as you are officially pronounced the "champ."

At this point allow yourself to spend a few minutes relishing what it is like to win. Try to recall times in your past when you have accomplished specific goals. Since the onset of panic disorder, you have probably experienced what it is like to lose more often than to win. Over and over again, your anxiety has proved itself to be the undisputed champion. Now you have finally taken away its title.

This specific visualization should be done frequently to reinforce your determination to triumph over the anxiety. Merely suggesting that you are strong and powerful without animation visualization will usually provide minimal results. The anxiety is subconsciously perceived as bigger, stronger and much more powerful than sufferers perceive themselves to be. Externalizing your anxiety and defeating it changes that perception.

Animation visualization can also be used for phobias, specifically animal and insect phobias. Visualize the particular object of which you are phobic as a cartoon. Then open your eyes and draw the cartoon on paper. After drawing the cartoon, provide it with a name, and personify it with a brief biography. The animal or insect becomes innocuous in this way, and soon you can use systematic desensitization with the cartoon. Eventually, you will be ready to place yourself in closer proximity to the actual animal or insect. As you approach, slowly, recall the cartoon and use the same names on your objects of fear. Then touch or hold the object just for a brief second and stop. Repeat this exercise several times until you start to feel more comfortable. Eventually, the objects you once feared may seem as harmless as a stuffed teddy bear.

Chapter 4

CONTROLLING AND ALLEVIATING SYMPTOMS

DIZZINESS

Dizziness is one of the chief complaints of panic disorder sufferers. There are many reasons for the symptom. Sometimes it is caused by vertigo, which is often associated with inner ear difficulties, altitude changes, and other factors. Or a person's blood pressure may fluctuate as a response to anxiety, causing dizziness (although such fluctuations are usually not significantly abnormal). Still, the slight shift can cause light-headedness and affect the semicircular canals of the inner ear, resulting in distorted messages from the eyes to the brain. Consequently, the ground seems to move in waves, buildings and cars sway, and the physical shapes and sizes of people, animals, signs, and other objects continually change. Dizziness also can result from changes in blood gases brought about by shallow breathing.

The most difficult challenge for the panic disorder sufferer is to not be intimidated by the dizziness. Of course, it is very difficult to continue talking, walking, driving, shopping, etc. when it feels as though your whole world is spinning around you. The tendency, of course, is to believe that the dizziness means that there is something terribly wrong physically and if you proceed with your activity the dizziness will increase until you lose consciousness.

To prevent this catastrophe from occurring, it may seem as if you have no choice but to go home immediately.

If you have received a medical evaluation and your doctor is satisfied that you are in good health, then most likely the dizziness is a symptom of your anxiety and not some neurological disorder that will cause you to faint at a most inopportune time. Here are a few tips to help you manage the dizziness when it occurs:

1.   Whether or not you have received a diagnosis of hypoglycemia, low blood sugar can cause you to feel dizzy. Eat a high-protein food every three to four hours and try to minimize sugar and caffeine.

2.   Dizziness is one of the tactics your anxiety uses to frighten you. The more attention you pay to the dizziness, the worse it will become. This is because the dizziness is being created by both an increase in adrenalin and shallow breathing. The most effective way to combat the sensation of dizziness is to "float" with it. Breathe deeply, close your eyes for a moment or two, grab onto something sturdy and simply let it happen. Floating with the dizziness will enable you to realize that it probably will not paralyze you and that if you can give yourself a little bit of time, it *will* pass. However, there is one situation in which floating is not recommended. This is when you have to remain in control. For example, when you are driving a car at high speeds, you cannot afford to "float." Instead, utilize the many tools at your disposal already described in this book. One effective technique is to use your anger at a critical moment when you feel the dizziness begin to overwhelm you. This will be discussed in a more elaborate treatment of freeway driving later in this chapter.

FEAR OF CHOKING

The fear of choking on food can be another symptom of panic disorder. In some cases, the fear exists because of a past incident that involved choking on food. The incident may have been experienced personally or created by another's choking situation. One client I treated for this problem had watched a parent choke on his food and nearly die in the process. Although this client was very young when the incident occurred, she had expressed feeling guilty that she did not do anything to help him. Many years later, she developed the fear of choking after successfully combating other symptoms associated with panic disorder.

Treatment was focused on helping this client to resolve her guilt and the utilization of both hypnosis, systematic desensitization and exposure therapy, but this is something you can do yourself. First, however, you may want to receive a medical evaluation to determine if there might be a physical cause. Sometimes disturbances of the esophagus and upper gastrointestinal tract or swollen lymph glands can create choking sensations. Once you have ruled out a medical cause, you are ready to begin.

Again, you may replace hypnosis with a progressive relaxation exercise. Having achieved a feeling of calm, identify your food hierarchy. There are bound to be those foods that appear to go down more easily than others. Your goal is to eventually imagine eating all foods, but you should start with the ones that are least threatening.

Visualize a bowl of clear lukewarm broth and a teaspoon. Observe yourself putting the teaspoon in your mouth and swallowing the broth. Continue to do this until it feels comfortable. Stop. Get up and make yourself a bowl of clear broth and finish it, using a teaspoon. You have completed the first part of this exercise. Now try to schedule some time to go to your favorite restaurant with a friend and order clear broth. Eat it slowly while engaged in conversation, but try to finish every last drop. If you manage this dining experience successfully, repeat the same relaxation exercise, using the food you identify as being lowest on your food hierarchy. Practice the same exercise and then prepare and consume the food immediately after you have completed the relaxation portion of the exercise. Once again, try as soon as possible to schedule time with a friend, go to a restaurant and order the same food. Continue to do this with all the foods in your food hierarchy. Subsequent to each mental exercise, make certain that you practice eating that identical food when you are with another person and away from home.

FEAR OF VOMITING

Like the fear of choking, some individuals have developed this phobia after an experience of being ill and vomiting in a public place uncontrollably. Interestingly, just as many people develop this fear without ever being subjected to such an experience. Like choking, a medical evaluation would be appropriate, particularly if the fear of vomiting is preceded by feelings of intense nausea. If a medical evaluation reveals nothing is wrong, then the following exercise may offer relief.

A fear of vomiting in public places often accompanies individuals who are overly concerned with the perception of others. Sometimes these same people suffer from social phobia. Of course, it is perfectly natural to be concerned about the way we think we look when we are actually having a panic attack. (Hair standing straight up, turning bright blue or green, eyes bulging out and looking as if we have landed from another planet.) The reality is, we do not really appear this way to others, but in the midst of such fear, it often feels like we do. Still, the major concern for panic disorder sufferers is not centered around how they appear to others but rather a fear that they are dying or losing touch with reality. To the individual who experiences the fear of vomiting, the fear of insanity is certainly a concern, but often it is less of a concern than the *embarrassment* that accompanies vomiting in public.

The fear of vomiting can be managed in several ways. First, it is helpful to use the IST exercises. Your negative thoughts may go something like this:

- "I'm afraid I'm going to be sick all over myself and everyone will stare at me and judge me."

- "I'm afraid once I'm inside the (train...plane...car) I'll get sick and be trapped and everyone will get angry at me."

- "If I start to vomit, I know I'll never be able to stop."

- "If I vomit, I'll get a panic attack."

Let us examine these cognitions more carefully. To begin with, you need to ask yourself how many times you have actually vomited? If you isolate the number of incidences, it is likely that they were infrequent. Perhaps the numbers range from zero to two. If you have never vomited, record that as a transformational thought (e.g., "even though I always believe I'm about to get sick, in reality I never have, not even once"). If you did actually become ill in public, what happened? Did people look at you with disdain and cast aspersions upon you for having such an obscene lack of impulse control? Probably not. After all, what would you think if you witnessed someone being ill? My guess is that you would feel compassion and concern for that individual. Perhaps you would not want to say anything that might embarrass that person. Or, you would offer assistance. Either way, your response would most likely not include anger or a perception that the individual who is vomiting must be mentally unstable. Anyone can get a virus or eat something that can cause vomiting. If you are still not convinced, you may wish to try a more aggressive approach to your fear of vomiting.

There are more effective methods involving a behavioral technique called "Flooding." Flooding has the potential to sometimes increase anxiety. The use of this technique for symptoms of vomiting should be restricted to a clinical setting where you can be carefully monitored by a licensed mental health professional.

CLAUSTROPHOBIA

Many people, with and without anxiety disorders, are uncomfortable in small spaces. Elevators, airplanes, MRI tests, etc. can cause very severe anxiety reactions. The type of anxiety disorder, however, will often determine the nature of the fear. For example, the panic disorder sufferer is likely to be frightened that once an elevator door has completely closed, an instant panic attack will occur in full view of everyone in the elevator. The individual with generalized anxiety disorder is less afraid of getting a panic attack in the elevator, but is usually fearful that the cables will break and the car will take a lethal plunge. The person with posttraumatic stress disorder may be convinced that someone on the elevator will have a gun. The person with claustrophobia fears that the elevator will get stuck between floors and no one will get there in time to be rescued from suffocation. Certainly you can see that the various scenarios are all different, yet equally terrifying.

If you have an appointment with someone whose office is in a tall building, it would be wise to visit the elevator one or two days prior to your appointment. Make this journey at an hour that is relatively traffic-free. Then, ride up and down the elevator several times to become familiar with its rhythm and speed. Often, elevators pause before they go to the next floor, and if that pause appears to be longer than expected, an interpretation may be made that the elevator is stuck. On the day of your appointment, catch the eye of another elevator passenger and smile. If you feel comfortable, engage him or her in a brief conversation and you will realize that you are not alone. Watch the floor numbers register to confirm that the elevator is indeed moving. If necessary, close your eyes for a few seconds and "float."

Some people find it easier to get off the elevator at every stop. If this helps you, do it. If the building is a skyscraper, bear in mind that in the time it takes for you to get on and off the elevator, it will probably have reached your floor. This is because elevators in tall buildings usually move very swiftly.

You probably have discovered that going back down the elevator is often much easier. You can look forward to going home. When you land on the first floor, take a moment to look at the elevator from a new perspective. Learn to see the elevator as your friend. After all, it saves you from traveling up so many stairs. Perhaps, in some way, you can come to regard the elevator as an ally instead of an enemy. It is also important to praise yourself for being able to ride in the elevator successfully.

Planes and Trains

Once that door shuts, you have made quite a commitment, especially on a train or plane. You cannot go screaming "turn around, I've changed my mind!" This is why so many anxiety sufferers are frightened of this mode of travel. As long as you believe you have an out, you will be in conflict as to whether or not you should be using your out. The conflict creates anticipatory anxiety until you either get a panic attack or exercise your option to leave. On the plane, there is no out; therefore, no conflict. You do not have any other option except to remain on the plane until it lands. No option, no point in being anxious. Simply sit back, read, talk to another passenger, listen to music, watch a movie. Stay involved with some activity and remember that if you feel the slightest wave of anxiety, you must assert "NO! NOT THIS TIME!" You cannot afford to be anxious, so you simply won't get anxious. Let the plane or train be your temporary home. Settle into it and relax.

Markets and Shopping Malls

Many years ago, you could go shopping for clothes, groceries, and various kinds of merchandise on nearly any street in open air. Open air markets still exist. However, the trend over the last ten years has been to build enclosed shopping structures. Even in California, where the climate is conducive to outdoor malls, there has been an emphasis on incorporating as many stores as possible and completing them in one huge, enclosed shopping structure. The larger the mall, the more prestige it is perceived to have. Anxiety sufferers find these malls intimidating and perceive them to be sprouting up by the hundreds, which could be one reason why catalog shopping and television shopping have proliferated. Not everyone is pleased with having to endure the crowds and maze-like structures of large shopping malls. Once in a while, there may be a valid reason for patronizing such a place, especially if home shopping cannot provide you with a particular product in time for a special occasion.

Grocery shopping is, of course, much more difficult to avoid. Although markets do often deliver, for the most part it is easier to be able to make your selections where you can see all of the merchandise. Whether you are in a large shopping mall or in a grocery store, there are several measures you can take to make yourself feel more comfortable:

1.   Wear sunglasses to minimize the glare from fluorescent lighting which can be very disorienting.

2.   Mark your progress incrementally. Do not attempt to do all of your grocery shopping or clothes shopping in one fell swoop. Decide on two or three items, locate the express lane, stand in it, reach for a magazine, and read it while you wait. Learning to distract yourself is critical when trying to challenge your anxiety. Fortunately or unfortunately, there is a great deal of stimulation in a market from which you can choose to distract yourself. If your legs or arms are still shaky, you may clutch onto a rail to gain balance. *Do not leave* despite your desire to flee. No matter what, pay for your items, and when you exit the market, provide yourself with many positive strokes. Do not let more than three or four days pass before you enter the very same market and purchase only a few items again in a short line. If the lines are extremely long, then you should leave. Go back at a time when you feel assured that you will not have to wait in line a long period of time. Your experience in the market may be somewhat uncomfortable but it should not be impossible. The idea is to make shopping a positive experience. Return to the same market every three or four days. Each time, add one or two items to your basket until you no longer qualify for the express (ten items or less)

line. Once you have passed through a regular line successfully,
then it is time to find a new store! Locate one fairly close
to home and begin the same way, a few items at a time. Always
practice IST, use your anger, and when you feel the need, float.
Your anxiety will soon learn that it has lost its influence over
you.

THE FEAR OF DYING

Many people with anxiety are convinced they are dying
when an attack occurs despite frequent reassurances from their
physician that they are in good health.

A woman can leave the doctor's office with a clean bill
of health. Yet, if a panic episode occurs, she can immediately
convince herself that death is imminent. The inner dialogue may
be something like this: "Oh, my God, it's happening now that
the doctor is gone! Wait, I'm fine, don't worry, there is nothing
wrong with me. No. The doctor hasn't seen me when I'm
having an attack. She's wrong! She's wrong! I can feel I'm going
to die, I feel weak and afraid. I can't stop it."

No matter how much this individual tries to persuade
herself that she is fine, she cannot shake off her impression that
she is dying, despite her doctor's assurances ten minutes earlier.
This sufferer has lost the ability to reason. But the reality is
that she can regain control. She does not have to give in to
the fear. The following exercise can help you.

First see your physician before you do the exercise below.
If your doctor has assured you that your health is good, ask
for an outline of the various tests you have taken and to write
down the findings. Keep this information with you at all times.
If for any reason the doctor has determined that you have some
health problems, it is vital that you know exactly what these
problems are, their symptoms, and the prognosis for their
development or remission, with or without treatment. If medication
has been prescribed, find out what the side effects are. Make
a list of these side effects and put it away. Do not refer to this

list again unless you experience a significant change in the way your body feels and reacts. When you take the medication, if your feeling matches a symptom on the list, telephone your doctor immediately with that information. Even if your symptom does not seem to correspond to the side effects on your list, you should still contact your doctor. However, be aware that you could be feeling a change because of an expectation that something bad will occur merely if you try a new medication. Follow the advice of your physician. If you still have difficulty, you may want to double check side effects with your pharmacist. You can even request a fact sheet from the pharmacist on that medication. But be careful. You will naturally have a tendency to believe that you will experience every possible side effect. You must be prepared to separate reality from imagination. Acquire the information you need, but do not allow yourself to become overly concerned and hypochondriacal.

Now that you have a clear picture of your state of health, it is time to change the tape. However, your first order of business is to face the truth. Death is a certainty. There is no way of knowing when, where, or how it will occur. Whether it occurs tomorrow or twenty years into the future, you must come to terms with the reality that dying is inevitable. Chances are that you never really thought about death until you developed your panic disorder. Now, unfortunately, you probably associate death with the feeling of insurmountable panic. So now is the time to begin to educate yourself about dying. Dr. Elizabeth Kubler-Ross has written several fine books on the death experience. I strongly urge you to read one or more of them. If you have a strong religious orientation, explore the beliefs of your religion regarding death and dying.

Once you accept that dying is a natural part of life, and that there is ultimately no escape from it, you may actually feel less anxious about it. The reason for this is that although you may have been able to provide yourself with rational reasons to explain why you are not dying during a panic episode, subconsciously you feel that if you do not die this time maybe you will die next time. In other words, it is necessary to bring yourself back to reality and recognize that you are safe but there may still be a part of you that guards against any assurance that death is ultimately avoidable. What you may now need to tell yourself is that "This time I'm fine. I'm not going to die, but if it is my time to die, I can only surrender." Develop a philosophy about dying that will serve you, not destroy you.

FEAR OF INSANITY

The fear of losing touch with reality and going insane defines panic disorder. This fear makes all other fears arising from this disorder pale by comparison. A physician can tell you that your heart is normal and temporarily put your fears to rest. However, during those moments when you believe that you have lost touch with the real world, no one seems to offer the kind of reassurance that allows you to feel truly safe. During a panic attack, you may feel as though you are being propelled out of your body at a great speed. You may see someone speak— that is, you see their lips move and hear sounds, but you cannot assimilate what is being said. You may even touch something but not know what it is you are touching. You may fear that if you go too far from home you may not be able to remember the route back; or, if you ask someone for directions, you will not be able to understand the directions.

What you are experiencing is technically called "states of unreality" or "dissociative states." These are listed in the manuals psychologists use to diagnose panic disorder. But panic disorder is not schizophrenia. It is not psychosis. A surprising number of people from all walks of life have had this disorder— people like you and me. As mentioned earlier, there is also a genetic predisposition to panic disorder. But the predisposition is to anxiety, not psychosis. *You will not go insane from this problem.* That does not happen—ever. (Nor can this disorder turn into psychosis.) For now, since your feelings of unreality may still appear at times, begin to accept them. You may feel disconnected. But so what? The truth is that in a real emergency,

if you have an external focus, you will be able to react
appropriately. Your preoccupation with your state of mind will
vanish the moment you need to rely on your mind to work for
you. Relax and use the deep-breathing technique outlined earlier
in this chapter. The increase in oxygen will make you feel more
centered. There are many other practical things you can do
to bring yourself back to reality.

FEELING "TRAPPED" IN THE
PRESENCE OF OTHERS

The worst thing about social situations is the fear that you
will be talking to someone, get an attack, and feel trapped
because you cannot let them know you are feeling anxious.

The more you try to cover it up, the more your anxiety
will intensify. Do yourself a favor and invent a reason to leave
such as, "I think I am having a reaction to some medication
I took. Please excuse me for a moment." Go to the restroom
and look into the mirror to assure yourself that you do not look
like you have just arrived from Mars. Then return and talk to
the same person, but this time make a concerted effort to hang
onto every word he or she says. Lose yourself in the conversation, knowing that you have the freedom to act a little
strangely because you have provided yourself with a legitimate
excuse. If the person asks what medication you took, you can
say it was anything—from a diuretic to a cold pill. It does not
really matter. The important thing is that you remind yourself
that you are not trapped. Permit yourself some leeway with the
truth to feel safe.

ANXIETY WHILE WALKING

Walking can be frightening because of shaky legs and
disorientation. Now that you know what causes shaky legs, you

might be less afraid and may be willing to walk outside your house. However, pick a specific destination before you begin. The destination should challenge you somewhat, but at the same time not overwhelm you. Select a point slightly farther than you are comfortable walking, then visualize yourself at that destination, feeling a great sense of accomplishment. Don't stop once you have started walking. Keep visualizing that goal and your smile of victory.

Sometimes, when walking becomes too difficult, running can reduce some of your shakiness. At the same time, it can help you to reach your goal more quickly. If you are in good health and have checked with your physician, run for a short distance. Then begin walking. You might also ask some of your friends to walk with you at first, or join a walking club until you are ready to go it alone. It is important that you eventually walk on your own and not allow yourself to find easy solutions in other people. Take your personal stereo and begin by traveling a little bit farther each day. If you wake up unusually anxious, walk the same distance you did the previous day. But if you do not go out at all, you will be setting yourself up to use avoidance the next day and the day after that. So keep moving.

If you are afraid that your anxiety will cripple you, know that, at worst, you can sit down at some convenient place until the panic leaves—usually in three to five minutes. Close your eyes, breathe deeply and slowly until the panic passes.

You can expect some labored breathing if you are walking fast or uphill. Breathing in this way provides your brain with increased oxygen, which can make you slightly light-headed for a few moments. This is a healthy thing, so do not worry. I would advise, however, that you do not take your walk when it is very hot or cold. I also recommend that you not exercise beyond your capability. Too much physical activity can sometimes create more anxiety. Be brave, but cautious, and do not become overzealous. Sometimes that can cause setbacks to occur.

THE URGE TO RUN HOME

There may have been many times when you have tried to travel a distance from home. Each time you were just about to reach the spot that was your goal, you told yourself, "I can't do this. I'm going home." Most likely, your anxiety stopped the moment you decided to turn around. Such is the nature of panic disorder. As you vacillate between moving away from home and returning home, tension mounts. Eventually the tension becomes so uncomfortable that it is easier to have a panic attack than to experience the tension. Thus, your fear of having a panic attack becomes the deciding factor, offering you a valid reason to return home. Once at home, you may feel relief for a while. But your subconscious mind is reinforcing the belief that you will never be able to leave home successfully. Each time you prevent yourself from reaching your destination, you add one more bar to your prison cell.

In order to free yourself from the anxiety that immobilizes you, you must be willing to put up with some temporary discomfort. The difference between discomfort and pain is that discomfort is unpleasant but not injurious. Pain, on the other hand, can be so severe that it can render you helpless. Fear is not pain. It is an uncomfortable sensation which may affect specific areas of your body and cause your imagination to run wild. But it cannot cause a heart attack, blindness, or insanity. Try the following exercise, with the awareness that discomfort is part of recovery.

Choose a location very close to your home. Close your eyes, breathe deeply and allow yourself to relax. Now imagine the location. Notice all the details of this place and the person if there is someone whom you plan to visit. Then visualize yourself at that location with that person, smiling with excitement at how comfortable you are. If you can see it, you can do it.

You will realize that when you plan to drive somewhere that causes you anxiety, you usually focus on the anxiety. Rarely do you focus on the destination. From now on, do not focus on the anxiety. Do not talk yourself into failure. Know that you can and will make it. Should you feel some discomfort, good! That means you are making headway. Your recovery is like the law of physics. For each action there is an equal and opposite reaction. Every time you make progress, expect some discomfort and welcome it with open arms. If you were not advancing, the discomfort would not arise to attempt to hinder you.

When you reach your destination, do not allow yourself to become complacent. Continue to plot new destinations, each one slightly farther away from the last. You must continue to expand your comfort zone as quickly as possible. The more often you push beyond your limits, the more self-confidence you will gain and the farther you will be able to drive.

You may still feel some concern about being a distance from home. For this reason consider investing in a cellular phone. This may seem like an extravagant expenditure. A cellular phone will give you the security of knowing that no matter where you go or how disoriented you might become, help is always near. As you probably experienced when you were anxious, the idea of having to stop and get out of your car was, and could again be, frightening. Consequently, a cellular phone can be considered a necessary tool. It can offer a tremendous sense of security.

If having a cellular phone is not possible, you may want to check with someone close to you and find out whether he or she will be home on the day you decide to challenge your radius. You will draw comfort knowing that someone knows where you are going and is available if you need help. This suggestion is applicable only to the *first time* you go a long distance from home. Otherwise, you may set yourself up to become dependent on others.

FREEWAY DRIVING

Expanding your comfort zone is no easy task. But once you have done it, you may be ready to drive on the freeway. Freeway driving is often the last frontier for many panic disorder sufferers because it involves being able to remain in complete control. If you get anxious on a side street, you can always pull over for a while until it passes. However, that is not possible on a freeway. This is why you must make certain that you have tried driving some distance successfully before you embark on this new and exciting adventure. If you are ready, here are some guidelines.

1.   Begin visualizing getting on a clear on-ramp and then see yourself driving with no one else on the freeway. Picture yourself seeing the next off-ramp and then exiting. You should observe a great big smile on your face, accompanied by a strong sense of accomplishment.

2.   Now it is time to take the challenge. Choose early morning hours on a weekend when there is almost no traffic on the freeway. Continue to visualize yourself getting on and off successfully. You will feel some butterflies in your stomach. This is good! Butterflies are really about feeling excitement rather than fear.

3.   Try to bear this in mind when you merge onto the freeway. Be determined in an angry way that you simply refuse to allow the anxiety to control you. If you feel it beginning to try its little tricks, curse, scream, and shout "NO!" This will allow the anxiety to back down immediately. Continue to drive until you see the next off-ramp and exit.

4.   Once you have completed this victory, do not minimize it. It is important to tell the people who have known about your disease what you have done and to celebrate your success with them.

5.   Do not return to the freeway until the next weekend at roughly the same time. You should repeat your same journey, going only to the first off-ramp in full view and then exiting. The next weekend, if you wish, you can go to the off-ramp directly past the one you had exited. Repeat exiting on that one before graduating to a farther one. Your progress should not be sabotaged by your impatience. Even if you believe that you are ready to take on a greater distance, it is important to repeat your success—twice—before graduating to a more distant off-

ramp. This is because the first time you surpass your parameters, you will always have a certain amount of anxiety and apprehension. The second time, you will probably be much more confident. It is important to associate driving with confidence, not apprehension. If you move too fast, you may deny yourself the opportunity to change your association of freeway driving with fear to an association with confidence. You should try to proceed gradually. The results will be well worth it.

SOCIAL ANXIETY

As you have already learned, it is not uncommon to have more than one type of anxiety disorder. Social anxiety is considered to be the most common form of anxiety and when it exists in combination with agoraphobia, it causes the individual to respond to a different set of triggers. For example, if you have social anxiety and have been reading earlier in the book about agoraphobics who find it difficult to leave home without a "safe person" to accompany them, you might be somewhat confused. This is probably because in your case, being around another person increases your anxiety instead of diminishing it. If you are like most social phobics, you may feel it is easier to have the option to panic when you are alone and spare yourself the pressure of having to act normal in the presence of another. The goal of an agoraphobic without social anxiety is to be able to expand the comfort zone alone. Your goal is to be able to expand your comfort zone while in the company of others. To achieve this, you may want to practice a technique called "**Emulation Therapy**."

Emulation Therapy is an approach I developed and have used successfully with social phobia. This approach can be traced to sports psychology. When a baseball player fell into a slump, no amount of coaching, cajoling or insight oriented therapy was helpful. This is because the athlete had temporarily lost his confidence after repeated failures. Eventually, the ball player perceived himself as a failure and with each strikeout, reinforced the belief that he was incapable of performing differently.

A sports psychologist suggested that the player pretend he is a great athlete with a super batting average. The ball player used this approach and his game improved dramatically. Eventually, this method became a standard practice for all types of sports.

The social phobic manifests a similar problem, but the sense of being a failure at socializing may span a lifetime. Some social phobics appear very shy and withdrawn, while others maintain a veneer of charming affability that masks deep discomfort. In either case, Emulation Therapy offers the social phobic a tool that both decreases anxiety and teaches communication skills.

Emulation Therapy is most effective when practiced in a very relaxed state. In Chapter 6, progressive relaxation is discussed. Review the section carefully. Once relaxed, try to choose the individual you will emulate. This person should be someone you perceive as comfortable socializing and has the ability to make others feel at ease as well. Wherever she goes, she seems to draw others toward her. She is self-possessed and is more interested in having a good time than worrying about seeking approval from others. If you do not know anyone like this, you may wish to select a character from a book or movie, or perhaps a celebrity whom you admire, and assume exhibits the qualities discussed. In your mind's eye, place this person at a party. Observe your emulation figure as she enters the room. Does she run to the nearest wall in an attempt to become invisible? Or rather, does she walk into a room expecting and desiring to be noticed? Are her eyes glaring down at the floor or is she making an effort to direct her glance toward others? When approached, what is her countenance like? Is she appearing aloof and distant or does she smile warmly as she is greeted? Study her eyes and lips. You will probably notice that the eye contact is penetrating and the mouth slightly open, suggesting a certain accessibility. Without communicating a word, she expresses a message that says, "engage me."

"But I don't know if I want to be engaged," you may be saying. Often social phobics feel exposed speaking to others, causing them to feel vulnerable. Or, in some cases, there is a concern that if they ask questions, they may be prying into that person's personal life. Another common experience is simply one of boredom. The social phobic often sees no point in exchanging what they consider to be superficial conversation. Socializing with someone whom they do not know seems like a waste of time and energy. Why bother to make small talk with someone if you will probably never see them again? If you are one of those people who find it difficult to socialize because, for the most part, you find people disinteresting and therefore become bored quickly, you may wish to learn more about something called Attention Deficit Disorder in adults. Often, a contributing factor to social anxiety is the inability to focus on another person. While anxiety can be responsible for a lack of concentration, individuals with ADD go a step beyond feeling anxious. They become so distracted, they turn off as the result of overstimulation. Social anxiety without ADD causes similar symptoms. However, utilizing Emulation Therapy consistently over a period of time can produce a successful outcome.

The Emulation Therapy does not stop with observation of your figure. To continue, you will want to imagine what it would be like to actually be that person. Imagine how you would feel entering a gathering cloaked in your emulation figure's body! After practicing this exercise in a relaxed state, you are ready to take the show on the road. Think of it as a secret game. When you interact with others, act as if you *are* your emulation figure and you may be surprised at how comfortable you feel and how differently others respond to you. Eventually, you may even begin to enjoy socializing and soon you will be able to own your social ease without having to pretend you are someone else.

A WAY OUT

It is important to know that, wherever you are, relief from your anxiety can be minutes away. This is why I recommend that you ask your physician for a small prescription of some antianxiety medicine. Just knowing that your medication is with you will give you a sense of security.

Chapter 5

DEPRESSION
AND ANXIETY

Most books targeted at anxiety focus on agoraphobia and panic disorder. This book is no exception. Most of the research, case histories and exercises herein are, in fact, designed with the agoraphobic in mind. This chapter, however, is designed specifically for the individual who suffers from Generalized Anxiety Disorder and depression. Generalized anxiety disorder (GAD) is mentioned much earlier in this book and is described as a form of anxiety which is usually less debilitating and often accompanied by depression.

Previously, in Chapter 3, discussion of the panic cycle illustrated the various peaks and valleys representative of panic disorder. The pattern is one of expectation and the source of fear is the fear itself. Panic attacks are characterized by the violent bombardment of physiological and psychological symptoms so severe they can be interpreted as dying or insanity. These episodes are typically triggered by something as simple as an idea, perception, or environmental change. The time it takes for a trigger to set off an attack can be as brief as half a second. In that moment, adrenalin can surge throughout an organism, appearing to render it completely helpless.

GAD often embodies a different set of fears. How these fears are conceptualized and the way in which the anxiety is manifested is also very different from panic disorder. With GAD, the anxiety is "free floating." In other words, there is an undercurrent of agitation. Panic attacks generally speaking, are not a source of concern. Rather, the anxiety takes the form of excessive worry. The concerns most commonly associated with GAD are those that are centered around health (specifically life-threatening illnesses), money, and in general, a mind-set that "eventually everything will fall apart." The GAD sufferer fears the loss of family, friends, job, health, status, etc.

The following composite illustrates GAD and depression: Courtney is employed at a large, executive law firm specializing in environmental law. Courtney graduated from an Ivy League school with a variety of academic awards and honors. Four of the largest law firms in the nation offered her positions with top salaries. She chose the firm that she believed had the best reputation for maintaining and advancing their employees. Courtney has worked at this firm for four years and has managed to generate a very large client base, billing far more hours than most of her colleagues. The senior partners have alluded to her future as a partner in the firm and she is regarded with a great deal of respect by her co-workers. Courtney has been married to a very loving, sensitive and handsome gentleman for about one year. Together, their incomes have afforded them the financial freedom Courtney had only dreamed about years ago. They travel, own their own home, have extensive clothes and jewelry, and live very well. Courtney's husband loves her very much.

But each night after they position themselves for sleep, Courtney lies awake for hours worrying about three things: 1) the periodic pain in her arm that to date has not been explained, 2) the belief that the partners at the firm plan to fire her and replace her with a male counterpart, and 3) that the pain in her arm will be diagnosed as breast cancer and when it does, her husband, Jeff, will finally leave her.

These recurring scenarios dominate much of Courtney's waking life as well as her sleepless nights. Courtney's fears are extreme. When she passes by an indigent person, she tells herself that someday she, too, will be homeless. Courtney has contingency plans for how she will survive in her car should she lose her job and her husband abandons her. These fears seem particularly irrational given that, with Courtney's legal background, she has certainly learned that, if there were a divorce, she would not be abandoned by the courts. In addition, if she were to lose her job at one firm, her experience and education would make her extremely employable.

Even so, Courtney cannot refrain from thinking obsessively about how she will lose everything she has. The anxiety that Courtney lives with might be tolerable if it were merely uncomfortable, but it causes her to feel depressed. Courtney experiences mild to moderate depression nearly all the time. She experiences acute depressive episodes two to three times a year.

Acute or major depression afflicts nearly eleven million Americans and the numbers of sufferers are growing. Major depression is most often associated with generalized anxiety. Although there have been some major breakthroughs in the treatment of depression with medication and specific types of psychotherapy, statistics indicate that the suicide rate has not declined. This could indicate several possibilities: among them, that the general population is not informed of the latest treatments for depression or it does not recognize the need for treatment.

In fact, depression is a disease that can seriously impair daily functioning. It afflicts twice as many women as men and like anxiety, there is a genetic predisposition. Other contributing factors are:

1. Substance abuse
2. Major life crises or change
3. Certain psychiatric disorders
4. Prolonged physical illness or degenerative disease
5. Certain prescription medications

The symptoms of depression include:

1. Fatigue
2. Hopelessness/helplessness
3. Feelings of unworthiness
4. Loss or increase in appetite
5. Difficulty concentrating
6. Tendency to isolate oneself
7. Feeling nonemotional or feeling overwhelmed by small problems and easily moved to tears
8. Unable to manage daily personal hygiene and/or household responsibilities
9. Sleeplessness or excessive sleep
10. Thoughts of suicide
11. Frequent headaches
12. Various body pains
13. Frequent colds
14. Impotence or lack of interest in sex
15. Memory problems
16. Anxiety

If you can identify with at least three of the symptoms listed between numbers 1 through 10 and have experienced these symptoms over two weeks, you may be suffering from a depressive episode. This may sound frightening but, actually, with the right treatment, the success rate for reducing or eliminating depression is very high. We will be discussing more about treatment later in this chapter.

Use this book as a resource to help you to conquer your fears and depression. However, as mentioned earlier, this book is not a replacement for professional evaluation and treatment. If you believe that you suffer from major depression, it is critical that you see a mental health professional. Living with anxiety may be uncomfortable, but it is not life-threatening. Depression can be very dangerous. Pep talks from well-meaning friends can sometimes accelerate a retreat into silence potentiating feelings of isolation and suicidality. If you are suffering in the manner described above, before turning another page, get professional help.

Another form of depression is called manic depression or bipolar disorder. Bipolar disorder has the following characteristics: 1) patients experience periods of euphoria, agitation and/or anxiety alternating with periods of deep depression; 2) they have a feeling of being "special" or "chosen"; 3) they talk very quickly and excessively but with difficulty focusing on a specific topic; 4) they are easily distracted, having racing thoughts; 5) they are compulsive in a variety of areas like shopping, sex, or gambling; 6) they can be easily angered, and escalate rapidly into a rage.

If this set of features seems familiar and you identify with at least three of the symptoms listed, you may have bipolar depression. If so, professional intervention is critical.

Depression and anxiety may appear to be entirely different disorders. But although the symptoms manifest differently, the development and progress of these diseases are strongly related. For example, perhaps you experience an episode of anxiety. It appears to be related to a specific crisis (e.g., the sudden death of a loved one). That episode may be terrifying, but it may never happen again. However, if the anxiety does recur, the chances of developing a panic disorder or other anxiety disorder are greater. Moreover, the greater the frequency and duration of the episodes, the more symptomatic one will become. Without treatment, the disease becomes a lifestyle, and in this way we perceive anxiety disorders and agoraphobia to be degenerative. Avoidance reactions, being reflexive, can soon become more familiar than nonavoidance behaviors.

Depression is a different animal with a similar bite. One episode of major depression following a crisis is, of course, no cause for alarm. Losing a loved one, a job, dissolution of a relationship, or any loss can cause a "reactive depression," which is very common. If the depression recurs for whatever reason, chances are higher that the individual may continue to experience episodic depression during transitional phases of his or her life. If the depression persists over many years, it may soon develop a life of its own and the person who used to "get depressed" may now, for the majority of the time, "be" depressed. There may be gradations in the symptoms, as is true of anxiety. However, without proper treatment, an individual who continues to experience episodes of major depression will probably develop a chronic depression that will usually only worsen. Like an agoraphobic, the depressed person isolates and maintains a constant stream of negative attitudes about the rest of his or her future. The depressed person talks him/herself into depression first, just as the agoraphobic talks him/herself into staying at home. Obviously, these internal dialogues are very unconscious and their impact often goes unnoticed. The depressed person is usually in so much pain all the time that he/she is not cognizant of the internal dialogues that reinforce the depression. Even many professional therapists, until recently, have been unaware of how to treat depression through psychotherapy.

PSYCHOTHERAPY AND DEPRESSION

Since the development of psychotherapy, the promise of treatment has always been to help the patient unravel those traumatic events in his/her life, and repressed fears, desires and beliefs, that prevent the patient from being happier and healthier. Schools of psychology and schools of thought have proliferated and developed their own unique theories and models for treatment. Most models are usually the result of a "psychotherapeutic orientation," and the interventions and techniques prescribed are specific to that orientation. The orientation is observed regardless of the cluster of symptoms that the patient presents. One of the most established psychotherapeutic orientations is what is called psychodynamic-based therapy. To put it briefly, psychodynamic theory attempts to heal the patient through facilitating dialogue about the past and enabling the patient to make appropriate associations between the past and what they may be presently experiencing. Of course, bear in mind I am attempting to condense a truly brilliant and elaborate psychotherapeutic system into two sentences. Psychodynamic theory is quite sophisticated and requires many years of specialized training to apply well. The majority of psychotherapists, indeed, are not specifically psychodynamic and may merely incorporate much of this theory and its practice into their work with patients.

Until recently, research on the effectiveness of psychodynamic approaches has been somewhat limited. At last, however, we now have some substantiated evidence that clearly eliminates the various treatment models that are not effective, and those that are most effective, for the treatment of depression and anxiety. As mentioned earlier in this book, therapies that focus on trying to solve the riddle of anxiety—that is, trying to locate a "cause"—are not as effective as the newer therapies such as cognitive behavioral techniques. Depression, according to recent research, responds similarly to cognitive behavioral therapy. We have examined how this works in the case of anxiety. Now, let us see how it can work for depression. One way to illustrate this is the following case:

Case Study: Derrick is a thirty-two-year-old man who has a longstanding history of depression. When Derrick was sixteen, he attempted suicide by a drug overdose. The attempt was foiled when his older brother interceded. Since that time, Derrick has been hospitalized several times by his therapist for symptoms of severe depression. Derrick entered treatment ten years ago. His therapist tried to help him identify the various problems he had faced while growing up. Derrick's parents had been very neglectful. His father was an alcoholic. Derrick was sometimes the victim of physical abuse. In therapy, Derrick came to understand how his rage at his father had been turned inward and caused him to become depressed. Derrick was given the freedom to yell, scream, kick pillows, and do whatever he needed to do to release himself from his rage. The therapist encouraged Derrick to confront his father. He did so, although reluctantly. His father even apologized for having had a bad temper. Derrick felt so much better for having confronted him. This all occurred in the first three years of Derrick's therapy.

Another aim of the treatment was to minimize Derrick's longstanding difficulties meeting women and being able to maintain relationships. In most cases, Derrick was terrified that he could never trust anyone he cared about. In his fifth year of therapy, Derrick fell in love, got married and started a family. He was employed at a company that was stable and provided him and his family with a middle-class lifestyle.

But in his sixth year of therapy, Derrick experienced an acute depressive episode requiring hospitalization and medication. No apparent stress precipitated the episode. Six different kinds of antidepressant medications were prescribed for him, but he could not tolerate their side effects, so medication was discontinued. At this point, Derrick began to experience a great deal of generalized anxiety and soon developed panic attacks so severe that it was all he could do to get himself to work and back home again. At this point, he sought therapy at the Institute.

When a patient presents symptoms of both severe anxiety and depression, it is usually recommended to treat the anxiety first, providing that the patient is not in danger of harming himself. At the time of treatment, Derrick was not suicidal, but he was very depressed. As I worked with Derrick, he learned to master his anxiety and his attacks rapidly diminished in frequency and intensity. Derrick began to feel better, although he still experienced moderate depression.

A discussion of depression earlier in this chapter describes the negative mind-set from which the depressed person operates. Researchers have recently noted that it is often contraindicated to ask a depressed person to recall painful events, as it only serves to reinforce that they are in pain. The conclusion the depressed person may draw is, "See, my whole life stinks, nothing will ever change."

Derrick's previous therapist *reminded him* each time he talked about his painful past, that he had always been suffering. Derrick's interpretation was that, since he had always suffered, he would only continue to suffer, that his depression was not inappropriate, merely exaggerated. This is not to say that a therapist should not address issues as they arise in counseling and that a patient should not be allowed to express feelings about those issues. However, in the case of someone who is experiencing a major depressive episode, cognitive behavioral interventions are recommended.

Derrick did receive cognitive behavioral therapy for his depression and within twelve weeks, his symptoms remitted.

TREATING DEPRESSION EFFECTIVELY

Depression can be treated in three ways: 1) medication, 2) psychotherapy, and 3) medication and psychotherapy.

In the case of mild depression or dysthymia, depression is often responsive to cognitive behavioral therapies. In the case of a major depressive episode—that is, if the individual's daily functioning is significantly impaired and thoughts of suicide are chronic—medication is usually indicated in addition to cognitive therapies. A complete guide to medication is supplied at the end of this book in order to help you understand the types of medications available. Of course, once again, it is important to be cautious and to seek professional help from a mental health specialist who will know when and if it is appropriate for you to take medication.

You have read the terms "cognitive behavioral" repeatedly in this book as it applies to anxiety. IST, Detached Observer, Anger As Power, are all specific techniques to change the way you relate to your anxiety. Just as a panic disorder sufferer is constantly convinced through negative self statements that all new experiences will create a panic episode, the depressive is no different. During moderate or severe depression, each thought, and each and every perception is based upon the premise that failure is imminent. Hope is something that is reserved for the lucky ones, those people who seem to get all the breaks and are loved by everyone. The depressive has an entire formula worked out, complete with a group of thoughts reserved for each and every occasion, and each of these thoughts clearly confirm why the depressed person will never achieve fulfillment. Moreover, the depressed individual is no longer driven by the basic survival instincts like eating, sleeping, sexual pleasure, etc. During a depressive episode, the sufferer is unable to experience anything that provides pleasure or even the desire to just survive. The plenitude of basic instincts that motivates humanity toward self-preservation—not to mention self-improvement—are gone. The depressed person then organizes his or her belief systems based upon an even more distorted view of life. The negative self-statements eventually replace all realistic perceptions of the world. Soon, all that is known about the prospect of living is that one more day will be painful, chaotic and hopeless.

One of the best ways to understand how a cognitive approach can help you change your distorted perceptions is by reading selections from some common dialogues I have had with patients. As you read my responses, you can practice being the therapist and see what ideas you can develop that may help your patient (you!).

Client: I got a really strange message from my boss. I'm sure he's planning to tell me I'm being laid off.

Therapist: How are you so sure that's what he wants to say?

Client: He's been in a really bad mood lately. I think I must have done something really wrong.

Therapist: How long have you worked at this company?

Client: Ten years.

Therapist: Ten years is a long time. Do you think you're any good at what you do?

Client: Yeah. I'm always being praised for my work and I've been promoted three times since I've been here.

Therapist: Have you had the same boss all along?

Client: Yes.

Therapist: Have you ever noticed that he's been in a bad mood before?

Client: Oh sure, sometimes.

Therapist: During any of these times that he was in a bad mood, did he tell you that he was angry at you or threaten to fire you?

Client: No, I guess not.

Therapist: Are you willing to entertain the idea, based on previous experience, that his moods sometime shift and it has nothing to do with you or your job performance?

Client: What if it's different this time?

Therapist: What if it's not?

Client: Then I would have gotten myself all worried over nothing again.

Therapist: Exactly. So are you willing to try on a new perception for awhile and see how it fits?

Client: I guess so.

Therapist: How about each time you begin to have this particular concern, you ask yourself the questions I have asked you? Answer them honestly, then present to yourself the alternative answers as to why your boss may be in a bad mood, and remind yourself it may have nothing to do with you.

Client: Yeah, I guess I can do that.

In this scenario, you will notice that I did not lecture the client or minimize feelings. In a collaborative effort, we explored a distorted perception and developed a new strategy to correct it. If these types of self-defeating thoughts are allowed to exist without intervention, they will often snowball and the depression will continue to get worse.

One may well assert that once the patient found out that she was not going to be fired, she would not be concerned anymore. But her potential firing was never the problem to begin with. This situation was merely one of dozens that elicited overconcern. Each time the client passed through a perceived danger unscathed, she almost always breathed a sigh of relief and convinced herself that she was just "lucky for now"—but wait until the next time. And so it goes for many sufferers.

The situation above is not all that different from that of the panic disorder sufferer who is terrified that she will be trapped in an elevator. When the elevator doors open and she emerges, she experiences relief but she usually convinces herself that eventually her luck will run out and she will become stuck on the elevator. Until she practices IST and other cognitive techniques, the panic disorder sufferer will almost always be entertaining all kinds of terrible possibilities.

Depression should be reckoned with in a similar manner. A dialogue, as illustrated above, between a therapist and a client can be an excellent tool for you to use on yourself. Just remember this formula: **ASK • ANSWER • ALTERNATIVES**

Applying the three A's to most situations can help you to feel better, but you need to practice them continuously to achieve maximum results.

For example, one of the chief complaints of depression is lethargy and lack of motivation. Suppose that for one month you have consistently stayed in bed each weekend, skipped showers, and allowed dishes and laundry to accumulate. Every Friday night, you promise yourself that come Saturday morning you will take on the household chores and get them over with. Saturday morning arrives and you go back to sleep until noon or so. Once you awaken, you stroll out to the kitchen, survey the damage and, feeling completely overwhelmed, retire to your room for the rest of the day. Phone calls are deferred to your voice mail, you have your food delivered, and you have rented your favorite movies the day before. This is a critical time in your depressive cycle. The more you avoid and retreat, the worse your depression will become. This is itself something you have already known, yet you still cannot seem to drag yourself out of bed. This is where the three A's can assist you. Your first thought is, "I can't get out of bed today".

ASK   Why not?
ANSWER   Your immediate answer may be "because I'm too tired."
ASK   Does staying in bed make you feel better?

ANSWER   Yeah, it gives me the rest I need.

ASK   So, you always feel better after staying in bed all day?

ANSWER   I feel better for awhile, then I feel guilty, then I get more depressed.

ASK   Do you want to feel better or more depressed?

ANSWER   Obviously, I want to feel better!

ASK   What, then, could be some alternatives to allow you to get the rest that you need but help you to not feel guilty, thereby generating more depression?

ALTERNATIVES:
1. Plan a goal of one task and finish it.
2. Take a shower.
3. Endure ten minutes of some kind of exercise.
4. Return at least one phone call.
5. Allow yourself to watch movies or relax the rest of the day.

In effect, you have made an activity schedule for yourself, one designed by you, for you, and with your needs in mind. You have crafted a plan that allows you to be constructive in such a way that you should not become overwhelmed. If you had attempted to take on the whole house, including bills, laundry, chores, etc., you would probably never have gotten started. It would all have seemed to be too much.

A realistic activity schedule such as the one described above is an excellent tool that should be utilized daily. Your feelings of powerlessness and low self-worth will diminish significantly once you feel a sense of accomplishment.

In addition to arranging activities that help you to organize your life, it is equally important to make time for pleasure. Of course, when you're depressed, creating pleasure may feel like a chore. But you are still bound to feel worse if you avoid the chore. Besides, certainly some things still give you joy. If you have trouble identifying what those pleasurable activities may be, refer to old journals and photographs to see what your life was like before you felt depressed. You may recover all kinds of fond and fun memories.

It is equally important that despite your fatigue, you attempt to make arrangements to "play" at least once a week. Arrange plans days in advance with a friend to go to the zoo, shopping, movies, whatever. Commit to allowing at least three hours a week for pleasure. No matter how tired you may feel, do not allow yourself to cancel your date. Once you have kept this firm commitment, you will find that you can take on your activity schedule without feeling so overwhelmed.

Once you have completed some items on your activity schedule, go to bed and sleep, read, watch movies, do whatever you wish. As long as you fulfilled some of your responsibilities and your commitment to pleasure, the rest of your time gets to be managed in whatever way feels best to you.

Keeping busy is an important part of managing depression. Especially important is thought containment. Every negative idea can spark more self-defeating behavior. Your distorted perceptions can occur automatically, like a reflex. Unless you learn to replace those thoughts with the three A's, you can trap yourself into deeper depression. Here is another example of how to use the three A's:

SELF-STATEMENT	I'm depressed, nothing will ever change, I may as well end it now, there is no point in prolonging my misery.
ASK	Have you ever felt this badly before?
ANSWER	Yes, many times. But I'm sick of it.
ASK	How did you cope with the depressive episodes then?
ANSWER	I forced myself to get on with my life and eventually they just passed.
ASK	So, you did experience feeling better?
ANSWER	Yes.
ASK	Since you have had relief before, do you think it's possible to feel better again?
ANSWER	I suppose.

ASK   What were some of the things that you
                        did before that seemed to help you
                        recover faster?

List past behaviors that were positive. These are alternative
behaviors.

1. The last time I went for acupuncture, it seemed to help
    a little bit.
2. I watched my diet and exercised.
3. I made affirmations and put them all over the house.
4. I went to a number of 12-step meetings and kept busy.
5. I would not allow myself to feel like a failure.
6. I bought a new car.

ASK   Clearly you cannot purchase a new
                        automobile every time that you are
                        depressed. However, is it possible to
                        repeat some of the other behaviors?
ANSWER   Yes.

Here again, you can see how easy it is to talk yourself
into feeling worse or better. Reminding oneself of methods that
helped in the past is an excellent way of instilling hope for the
future. Self-dialogue is a very important method for helping
depression. Another valuable tool is hypnosis. At our institute,
we use hypnosis to treat both anxiety and depression. Hypnosis
may sometimes be difficult to master and is not for everyone.
It can, in some cases, bring up repressed feelings and emotions
one may not be prepared to deal with without help from a
professional. There is, however, an effective and safe alternative—
visualization. Earlier you read how visualization is used to treat
anxiety. Although the scenarios and content may differ slightly,
the process can be applied to your depression.

VISUALIZATION

Techniques for breathing and relaxation are already provided
in Chapter 3. Once you are relaxed, you can choose from a

variety of scenarios or design your own. These scenarios are designed to reprogram your negative cognitions to positive ones. Simply stated, imagery can realign your mind-set so that your perceptions are accurate instead of distorted.

Since you are the architect of your imagination, you should design scenarios that are comforting and sensually alive. The pictures you create should compliment your directives so that you can accept them more readily. In other words, use images that represent your style of thinking and reflect only the most positive feelings.

SCENARIO AND SUGGESTIONS FOR REPROGRAMMING

If you review your life, you will notice particular periods that were especially painful. Beginning with childhood, try to identify all the times that you felt rejected, neglected, criticized and alone. Recall vividly how that pain would get reinforced over and over again throughout your childhood and into adolescence. By the time you were a teenager, you may have already formed a negative identity—an identity that was built upon criticism and neglect from people who were supposed to support and encourage you. You may have learned, as you matured, that your needs were considered insignificant, and then interpreted that to mean that you were insignificant.

You then may have labeled these beliefs as "depression," which meant that you stopped believing in yourself and in your abilities and developed projections and formulations about your present and future. But your interpretation of reality is based upon events that occurred years ago. The inertia and hopelessness you feel now may be very real but they are merely manifestations of false beliefs and distorted perceptions. The good news is that you can now actually reformulate those beliefs. This, in turn, will allow you to see the world more clearly.

In order to do this, it is important for you to be able to discern the pain that you have truly suffered from that which you have erroneously suffered. Go back into your childhood again. Examine the incidents that caused your pain. Separate the types of pain in your mind—the neglect, fear, anger and so forth. If you have experienced trauma such as witnessing a parent being battered, or if you were physically or sexually abused, see it in your mind's eye and let yourself have your emotions. You may need to cry, or kick or scream. Allow your body to feel and do what comes naturally.

Now, when you're ready, put these emotions and the incidents that evoked them into special little boxes. You can use different colored boxes for the various types of pain. For example, put all the criticisms you internalized into a gray box; all those times you were frightened of being abandoned or injured into a black box; and continue to identify different emotions and supply different colored boxes for each. The boxes should all have locks and keys that belong to you.

Now, with all of your pain in the appropriate boxes under lock and key, you should notice that your mind is a little more clear and ready to receive new information. The information that you need to receive are suggestions that will help put your life back on track and provide you with a feeling of confidence and power. So, in order to give you back the power that you (believed) you lost, think of one place or activity where you feel okay. You do not need to feel perfect or exceptional, just okay. You can feel that okay in every situation if you will repeat and accept the following suggestions:

1.   You will no longer accept the most negative inter-pretations for any situation that disturbs you. Instead of jumping to the worst possible conclusions, you will find at least two other alternative explanations that do not involve a negative statement about your abilities.

2.   Visualize certain situations that particularly make you feel bad about yourself. Then watch the same situation occurring while responding differently. Notice that your response is coming from a place of self-confidence instead of self-loathing.

3.   In relaxation, practice this scenario at least one time per day, more if you have time. You may not be able to

consistently accept these affirmations but at an unconscious level you may, and eventually these new messages will be absorbed into your conscious mind until you notice that your depression has improved.

Depression is a pervasive and disabling disease. It is my hope that many anxiety sufferers who also experience depression in varying degrees will utilize the information and tools provided herein to hasten self-recovery. Once again, it cannot be underscored enough how potentially dangerous depression can be. There are many reasons why depression occurs, but one fact remains clear. Gone untreated, depression can result in suicide. If you or someone you love is suffering from major depression, get help at once. The patient's prognosis is excellent if he/she is treated properly. If you need assistance, there are referrals located at the end of this book.

Chapter 6

OTHER EFFECTIVE TECHNIQUES

JOURNAL WRITING

Journal writing involves recording your feelings and activities on a daily basis. It is common for people in twelve-step programs, such as OA and AA, to keep a journal. Journal writing offers a safe, nonjudgmental forum for expressing your most closely-guarded emotions. Panic disorder sufferers are often so distracted by anxiety that they may lose touch with how they feel and think about other aspects of their lives.

Writing your feelings down on paper can help maintain a more well-rounded self-perspective. Anxiety can appear to manifest "out of the blue." Yet if you can write down some of your thoughts previous to the onset of the anxiety, you may be able to see how you have talked yourself into becoming anxious. You may become familiar with your thought progressions and learn how to change such thinking into more rational and realistic expectations.

For example, suppose you are experiencing some intense anxiety. As you write down each thought, you remember that you watched a talk show about a man who had Lyme disease, a disease contracted from ticks. This man discussed his symptoms, which included weakness and lethargy. Shortly after this program, you had your panic attack. As you write, you realize that you began to subconsciously give yourself the message that you probably had Lyme disease. Up to now, your doctor had been merely unable to diagnose it. You think that a red mark on your leg looks suspiciously like a tick bite. You start to feel weak and lethargic. Your vision is blurring. You know the scenario. You scare yourself into believing the worst until you cause your own panic attack.

As you record your thoughts, you see the way in which you have frightened yourself. You can then create more realistic statements. For example, "Okay, Lyme disease involves a particular type of mark. I do not have that mark. I never saw a tick. I haven't been near any lush vegetation for a year. I was recently examined by my physician and there was nothing abnormal in my blood test. I can always get a specific test for Lyme disease if I develop other symptoms. Until then, I will think about something else." These are factual statements which you can write down, read and reread until you believe them.

Journal writing also allows you to log your diet and physical state of being. Let us say that you have not had much sleep for several days. You have been drinking caffeine to overcome drowsiness and ingesting excessive amounts of sugar for added energy. Suddenly, you start to feel anxious and cannot understand why. You skim your journal and read about how tired you were and the caffeine and sugar ingested. At once, you realize that you are anxious for a good reason. By now you have come to understand that fatigue and caffeine are strong contributors to panic attacks. Each time you understand more about a particular pattern that influences your panic, you will gain greater self-acceptance and learn how to change such patterns.

MASSAGE

Massage is therapeutic for several reasons. First, it gently coaxes your muscles into relaxation which, in turn, slows down your heart rate and allows you to breathe more deeply. As you have learned, hyperventilation can exacerbate and often create a panic attack. It is crucial that you find ways to regulate your breathing.

Massage supplies the muscles with increased blood flow and oxygen, thereby stimulating the brain to release endorphins (natural biochemicals similar to opiates). Endorphins can induce a very tranquil and almost euphoric feeling.

During anxiety attacks, you may notice that disorientation seems to make you feel like you are moving away from your body and the world in general. Massage serves to ground you by putting you in touch with your body. People report that during a panic episode they feel as though they are literally disappearing into thin air. Massage is a way of reminding you that you haven't "gone anywhere."

MEDITATION

I have already discussed the benefits of hypnosis. The difference between meditation and hypnosis has to do with intent and passivity. With hypnosis, you are providing yourself with specific imagery and instructions. The intention is to change your anxiety. *Meditation has no goal nor direction. It is more general.* There are many ways to move into meditation, many of which use imagery. However, the key to staying in the meditation is to allow your mind to decide your experience for you. This means that you need to relinquish expectations and control. If you trust that your mind knows where it wants to take you, then meditation can be a valuable tool for self-relaxation and spiritual development. Both hypnosis and meditation require a certain trust in your ability to maintain sanity. In hypnosis, you are simultaneously being active and passive, so you feel that you have control. You should experiment to decide which method works best for you.

If you choose to try meditation, you may want to use the following method.

1.   Lie down in a dimly lit room.

2.   Begin breathing slowly. Inhale through your nose and release slowly through your mouth. Make certain that you are breathing at your normal pace. Concentrate on the sound of your breath while you tell your mind to take you wherever you need to go. You may see various images. Follow those images. Most importantly, do not try to force your experience. Meditation feels different to each person. Try not to think about how it "should" feel or whether you are doing it correctly.

3.   After a short time, you may notice that your body seems heavy. You may move in and out of wakefulness. This means that your consciousness is reaching a higher state. No matter how relaxed you become, you will always be able to open your eyes and know exactly where you are. You may also sense some strong emotions emerging—you may even cry—but be aware that this is a process of cleansing. Tears are a way your consciousness helps you to let go and purify yourself.

During meditation, you may recall experiences from your past. These memories may seem larger than life. If this happens, allow yourself to express the emotions surrounding the memory or experience. Permit your active analytic mind to become passive. Move through your experience without the limitations placed on you by your own skeptical thoughts. Meditation does not have to be dramatic to fulfill its purpose. Simply allow it to flow naturally.

EXERCISE

"Exercise! you'll feel better!" How many times have you heard these words? I imagine quite a lot. This is because exercise is recommended for everything from depression to heart disease. There is a good reason why exercise is so highly regarded. This is because exercise 1) strengthens the muscles in the body, 2) improves circulation, 3) builds stamina, generating more energy, 4) tones the lymphatic system, allowing the body to cleanse itself of toxins, and 5) aids in digestion. In addition to all the physical benefits produced by exercising regularly, there are emotional and psychological benefits as well. Because the body and mind are so closely connected, when the body is fatigued, anxiety is more likely to occur. The increased energy resulting from daily exercise can help prevent fatigue. In addition to helping you become less tired, here are some other reasons why exercise is so important:

1.   You can increase your self-esteem through discipline and feeling fit.

2.   Depending upon the type of exercise, you can strengthen muscles and limbs, which will feel less shaky when you are anxious.

3.   Exercise normalizes breathing (in most cases). Shallow breathing becomes deeper and more regulated.

4.   Exercise stimulates substances in the brain called "endorphins." The chemical structure of endorphins is somewhat similar to that of opiates, a substance that produces a feeling of euphoria. The stimulation of endorphins often results in feelings of well-being. For an individual who is prone to bouts of depression, such a feeling is the difference between being depressed and not being depressed.

It would appear that exercise is good for everybody. However, that is, in fact, not the case. Exercise in many people eases tensions and feelings of depression; but it can, depending upon the exercise and individual, actually *increase symptoms of anxiety.*

Case Study: Suzanne entered treatment for a longstanding depression for which she had been seeing another therapist. Suzanne's therapist insisted that her depression would get better if she would begin each day with a brisk walk or jog. Like many individuals who suffer from depression, Suzanne had GAD.

Suzanne desperately wanted to overcome her depression, so she embarked on a rigorous exercise program for approximately three months. Each time she would exercise, Suzanne noticed that she felt even more depressed afterward. She reported this to her therapist, who assured her that the only reason she felt worse was because she was probably out of condition.

Determined to feel better, Suzanne persevered with her exercise program. She noticed that not only was her depression getting worse, but so was her anxiety. During the three months that Suzanne exercised rigorously, she began to have panic attacks almost on a daily basis and always immediately following exercise. It was at this point that Suzanne sought help at the Institute.

Our initial consultation always includes very specific questions about the patient's medical history, as well as inquiries into potentially anxiety-producing situations. During our first visit, I learned that Suzanne's mother had always been asthmatic and that Suzanne herself had seasonal allergies. I also learned that Suzanne felt worse in hot weather. If she is outside when it is very warm, she usually feels anxious. I had referred Suzanne to a cardiologist, who had diagnosed her with MVP. I have referred to this malady earlier in this book, as you may recall.

MVP is a slight abnormality of the heart which can cause an irregular heartbeat as the blood attempts to funnel its way across the heart walls with an impaired valve. MVP can cause shortness of breath which, in turn, can cause fatigue, as the body works twice as hard to help the blood flow evenly. MVP is not dangerous and many people may not know they have it.

In Suzanne's case, her cardiologist attributed her depression and anxiety following exercise to her MVP. Does this mean that Suzanne should never exercise again? Certainly not. However, in addition to having MVP, she, as mentioned earlier, is highly allergic. When Suzanne started her exercise program, it was late spring and all types of pollen swelled the air. Suzanne's allergies, coupled with the heat, intensified her breathing difficulties.

For this reason, Suzanne's cardiologist recommended swimming. Suzanne did live near a pool and once she began her swimming regime, she noticed that her energy increased and her depression and anxiety decreased. Suzanne did not swim straight laps; she often took her time, frequently just floating on her back and enjoying how calm and tranquil she felt in the water. When she did stroke, she made certain that she regulated her breathing so that she did not work too hard to breathe. The water also acted as a buffer between Suzanne and the pollen in the air. Also, Suzanne made sure she never stayed in the water longer than was comfortable.

This case history is significant because it illustrates the necessity for recognizing individual differences. Consequently, before embarking on an exercise program, you should go through the following checklist:

CHECKLIST

	Yes	No
1. Is your anxiety worse in hot weather?	___	___
2. Have you had a medical exam in order to rule out heart problems, respiratory problems, the Epstein-Barr virus, or other maladies?	___	___
3. Do you suffer from seasonal allergies?	___	___
4. Does exercise make you feel worse?	___	___
5. Are you comfortable exercising outside your home?	___	___

Examine the checklist closely and look at some methods that allow you to exercise comfortably. If you answered "yes" to question No. 1, then it is clear that you should not exercise in hot weather. Indeed, many panic disorder sufferers experience more anxiety when it is hot.

If you have answered "no" to question No. 2, then you should correct the problem before exercising. Heart disease, respiratory problems and Epstein-Barr virus are common diseases often made worse by too much exercise. There are many other diseases that may also present a problem during rigorous exercise, so *always consult with your physician first.*

If you have answered "yes" to question No. 3, then you may want to exercise or swim indoors.

Regarding question No. 4, if exercise makes you feel worse, see if you can isolate why. If none of the other items on the checklist apply, you may need to do some further investigation. You may be physically unfit and therefore need time to slowly build up your stamina. If you are significantly overweight, you may encounter special difficulties. First, you may find it more difficult to move around. Secondly, if you have feelings of shame about how your body appears to others, you may feel both self-conscious and resentful. Overweight individuals are often made to feel as if they "should" exercise; if they do not, they are then perceived as being lazy. Exercise can become a bitter medicine that society wishes them to swallow. Attempting to meet the expectations of those around you by engaging in something you dislike doing will only make exercise an arduous and joyless task. Under these circumstances, of course you may feel worse! If this situation feels familiar and you believe this is the reason why you have difficulty exercising, then an attitudinal change is in order.

You should exercise because it can help you to get over your anxiety quicker. Do it only for that reason, not because society will disapprove of you if you do not. You deserve to be free from your anxiety. Give yourself permission to *take care of yourself.* The next time you attempt to exercise, pace yourself and remember that you are doing it for no one else *but you.*

The last question on the checklist is very important. If you are uncomfortable going away from home, then you may need to exercise indoors, where you feel safe. After you have utilized some of the techniques offered later in this book that help combat anxiety, then slowly venture away from your home. Until then, perhaps you can exercise to a workout video— preferably one that is designed for your level of fitness.

Now that we have explored ways in which to safeguard you from the potential hazards of exercise, it would be useful to determine which is appropriate for you.

ANAEROBIC	AEROBIC ACTIVITIES
Weight Training	Swimming
Yoga	Walking/Treadmill/
Isometrics	Power Walking
	Running/Jogging
	Bicycling/Fitness Cycle
	Tennis/Racquetball
	Skiing/Sledding Hiking

Both types of exercise are beneficial for different reasons. It is usually advisable to start very slowly with one type of exercise, monitor your comfort, then add a different kind. Both aerobic and anaerobic exercises provide excellent therapeutic results. However, those results are quite different. The following chart explains features and purposes of the types of exercise within each category:

ANAEROBIC	AEROBIC
Increases muscle strength	Increases heart rate
Increases muscle size	Strengthens heart
Sculpts the body, depending upon concentration of specific muscle groups	Increases lung capacity
	Increases circulation
Can cause more of a "bulky" appearance and increase body weight	Contours your body
	Causes weight loss
Increases stamina	
	Produces endorphins
Increases oxygen supply	Increases stamina and energy

Whichever type of exercise you choose, you should be prepared to experience the following sensations:

ANAEROBIC	AEROBIC
Light-headedness	Dizziness
Rapid heartbeat	Rapid heartbeat
Shortness of breath	Rapid and loud breathing
Sweating Shaky arms and legs	Sweating
Occasional twitches, even up to several hours afterward	Increased energy; you may even feel "wired"
Muscle pain and sometimes limited range of motion for up to several hours after exercising	Warm face, often producing a flushed appearance
	Hot, thirsty. Shaky feeling all over the body after exercising

For now, we will assume that your physician has approved your exercise regime. *Unless your doctor has expressed a concern that your pulse must be consistently monitored*, I recommend that *you do not pay attention to your pulse rate.* If you become too aware of your pulse rate, you may run the risk of encouraging negative thoughts that lead you to believe that you must be having a heart attack. If you exercise correctly, your heart muscle will be working hard and your pulse will become rapid; your specific pulse rate is of secondary concern. If you follow the safeguards outlined earlier, you may find exercise very rewarding on many levels but most directly, it will help alleviate your anxiety. Before choosing a type of exercise, you should keep a few things in mind. First, both aerobic and anaerobic exercise work out your muscles and produce lactic acid. Earlier in this book I made mention of the relationship between sodium lactate (lactic acid) and anxiety. An overproduction of lactic acid can *increase* anxiety. You must remember to be very gradual in your exercise approach—never allow your muscles to become too sore, or you may find your anxiety increasing. Of course, sometimes becoming sore may be unavoidable, but it does not automatically mean that a panic attack is on the way! Drink extra fluids, rest, and never exercise the same muscle groups every day. Alternate between your upper and lower body if you are in weight training. If you are jogging, walking or even swimming, it is advisable to do it every other day for no more than twenty minutes until your muscles are able to accommodate more exercise.

Chapter 7

ALTERNATIVE APPROACHES

ACUPUNCTURE

I have already recommended massage as a possible adjunct to your self-help approach. Acupuncture can also be an aid to recovery.

It is not necessary to understand how acupuncture works in order for it to be useful. Suffice it to say that there are various organs in the body that govern certain emotions. There are specific meridians and acupuncture points which can direct your body's natural energies to heal organs or other parts of your body.

In acupuncture, fear is associated with the kidneys. An acupuncturist can use needles to promote the healing of kidneys. For the most part, acupuncture is painless. The thin, pliable needles of the acupuncturist are usually inserted quite superficially. They usually remain inserted for fifteen to twenty minutes.

People often experience a relaxed feeling during treatment. Acupuncturists refer to this as "floating." Sometimes it can feel almost euphoric. It is a feeling of total calm, much like the state one achieves during meditation. Often the patient will fall asleep during an acupuncture treatment.

If you decide to try acupuncture, you will probably want to see a practitioner close to home. However, do not allow distance to dictate your decision about whom you select. Just like other practitioners, some acupuncturists are better trained than others. Choose an acupuncturist who understands your particular needs.

HOMEOPATHY AND HERBS

Homeopathy is a natural approach to treating a variety of ailments that range from muscle sprains to insomnia. The homeopath uses remedies that are derived primarily from plants and minerals in order to stimulate the body's own healing process. The goal is to correct the imbalance that caused the ailment. Medication can cause you to experience side effects or idiosyncratic reactions; the remedies used in homeopathy are no exception. Although side effects from homeopathic remedies are rare and almost never permanent or dangerous, it is important to be aware that you can have reactions to such remedies. One of the more common reactions is heart palpitations, which will usually abate once the remedy is discontinued. Occasionally, symptoms may worsen at first, then remit as your body adjusts to the treatment.

Although there is no scientific method as yet to measure its effectiveness, some believe that panic disorder can be helped with homeopathy. *Calcarea carbonica* is a homeopathic remedy derived from oyster shells. It is often prescribed for the treatment of panic attacks. This remedy appears to be helpful for people who fall into a particular physical and emotional category.

For example, someone who is very hardworking and feels overwhelmed by responsibility may respond better than a person who lives a less structured, less demanding life. In homeopathic medicine, there are specific physical symptoms associated with the hardworking type. These symptoms include fatigue, joint pain, congestion, asthma, PMS, sinus congestion, and excessive perspiration. When calcarea is prescribed, some people report less anxiety and fewer panic episodes. There are many other remedies used to treat panic disorder—ask only an experienced homeopath to recommend them.

Saint John's Wort

Hypericum Persoratum or Saint John's Wort is an herb used to treat mild to moderate depression. It has been used in Europe successfully for many years. Studies report that, for depression, Saint John's Wort is an effective antidepressant with less side effects than conventional ones. The side effects that were reported on Saint John's Wort included allergic reactions, fatigue, gastrointestinal complaints, photophobia, and restlessness. Some of these side effects were dose related and in some cases disappeared when less of the herb was ingested. The therapeutic dosage for Saint John's Wort is still being investigated but experts suggest that 300 milligrams, three times a day, may be the optimum dose. Additionally, the herb should not be taken in conjunction with antidepressant medication, MAOI inhibitors or diet drugs. The effectiveness of the herb for mild to moderate depression is quite impressive. The majority of studies has focused on the efficacy of Hypericum for the treatment of mild to moderate depression.

The effectiveness for panic disorder is still being evaluated. However, the herb does appear to possess antianxiety properties and in some cases has been reported to relieve anxious symptoms.

Ginkgo (Ginkgo Biloba)

Ginkgos are the oldest living trees in existence. The leaves produced by this tree produce a substance called Ginkgolides. In Germany, the leaves are extracted and synthesized for medicinal purposes and have been used for over twenty-one years. It has been prescribed for dizziness, hearing loss, memory difficulties, circulatory disorders, headaches and fatigue. In the United States, Ginkgo has been promoted as a memory enhancer and natural antidepressant. While this herb is considered to be effective for depression, it has stimulating qualities which may actually increase anxiety.

Passion Flower (Passiflora Incarnata)

In Germany, Passion Flower is sold as a drug for nervousness and insomnia. It is reported to possess sedating properties and is often combined with other herbs to be used in compounds to eliminate anxiety. The effectiveness for panic symptoms has not yet been scientifically substantiated although some people report that it appears to minimize anxiety symptoms.

FOOD ALLERGIES AND IMPROVED NUTRITION

Earlier in this book, allergies and their effect on anxiety were discussed along with many other contributing agents. The relationship between food allergies, nutrition and anxiety merits further elaboration: The connection between all three is vital if we are to treat anxiety effectively. Food allergies can be so severe that a number of researchers now believe that they may play a key role in many kinds of maladies, from migraine headaches to multiple sclerosis. You may be asking yourself, "How do I know if I suffer from food allergies? How am I to be treated if I do?" There are a variety of methods used to assess food allergies and sensitivities. Some methods are considered more reliable than others. Some are newer than others, creating some doubt as to their effectiveness by conservative practitioners. For example, one of the more traditional ways to be tested for general allergies is to visit an allergist. An allergist will most often use a technique called a "scratch test," where small amounts of various allergens suspected of eliciting your allergic responses are delicately applied subcutaneously. Then the skin is carefully observed in anticipation of a reaction.

If no reaction takes place, the diagnosis is that the patient is not allergic to that specific compound. Conversely, if some redness and swelling occur, the patient is diagnosed as being allergic. If the allergic reaction is initiated by environmental stimuli such as molds or pollens, then, usually, antihistamines can be prescribed, or small amounts of the substance to which the patient is allergic can be injected. The latter procedure is used toward the goal of making the person's immune system tolerate the allergen.

Scratch tests are considered to be very reliable for detecting environmental allergies. Their reputation for detection of food allergies, however, is not exactly sterling. In fact, unless an allergy is severe enough to cause vomiting and rashes, it will often remain invisible during a scratch test. The absence of a reaction will offer false reassurance to patients that they are able to consume the tested food without difficulty. In fact, this may not be true.

Consequently, other forms of allergy testing have been developed and utilized in an attempt to offer more sophisticated diagnosis. These include blood tests, kinesiology, pulse testing, and the slow insinuation of various foods, after fasting, to see if a reaction takes place. All of these tests have their pluses and minuses, but overall they are better at identifying allergies than a traditional scratch test.

The most common foods implicated in allergies are eggs, milk, chocolate, beef, potatoes, wheat, shellfish, nuts, and corn. The symptoms most often accompanying ingestion of these foods include nasal blockage, headaches, irritability and anxiety, tachycardia, nausea, lethargy, dizziness, vertigo and asthma. If an individual is already predisposed to panic disorder, it isn't difficult to see, even if he/she has a conventional diet, how hard it may be to stop anxiety from erupting into full blown panic episodes. The question still remains. How does one treat a food allergy effectively?

In order to treat food allergies and oversensitivities effectively, it is helpful to know more about what an allergy is and how it develops. Various theories exist to explain allergies. However, since this section focuses on alternative health care, it would be most germane to explain allergies from a perspective that departs from a traditional medical model.

The latest research in nutrition and mental health has indicated a strong relationship between the depletion of B vitamins and anxiety. In fact, in his book *Nutritional Influences in Illness*, Dr. Melvin Werbach has cited numerous studies supporting this unusual relationship.

I recall my own experience nearly fourteen years ago, when a nutritionist put me on a regime of B-vitamins to be taken three times per day. Each time I took my dosage of vitamins, I had the same sensation that I would get from too much caffeine. My heart would race and I felt disoriented and anxious. This would occur within thirty minutes after taking the vitamins. Eventually the regimen became so difficult that I stopped taking the vitamins, at which point the symptoms abated. Of course, I never told my nutritionist, assuming he would be skeptical. After all, I was anemic and B-vitamins were certainly indicated. It never occurred to me that my reaction could have been an allergic one. But I soon learned of the relationship between anxiety and allergies. I realized that I was allergic to B vitamins. In fact, longstanding allergies can frequently trigger other allergies; this makes it nearly impossible to avoid the foods to which one is allergic.

In his book *Food Allergies And Nutrition,* James Braly, M.D. details his studies with patients suffering from various food allergies.[4] Dr. Braly cites numerous studies correlating food allergies with overstimulation of the adrenals.

The adrenals, as you may recall, are located at the top of the kidneys and produce adrenalin. Earlier in this book, I discussed the relationship between excess adrenalin and anxiety. Studies confirm that people with panic disorder often secrete too much adrenalin. According to Dr. Braly, food allergies may contribute signifi-cantly to this problem. Unfortunately, the adrenals are a necessary organ for maintaining a healthy immune system. If the adrenals are exhausted from overstimulation, it becomes even more difficult for them to regulate the immune system, thereby increasing allergic reactions and, in turn, stressing the adrenals even more.

Once a person's body becomes sensitive to allergens, mental and emotional states cannot be separated. Common irritants such as tobacco can impair one's ability to think effectively. In addition, there are specific allergies of the brain, called "brain allergies." They occur when the brain is the target of specific allergens. The brain's delicate biochemical balance can be disrupted, causing depression, anxiety, insomnia, and even phobias.

In his book, Dr. Braly provides a case study of a woman who suffered from food allergies as the result of living in a dormitory. The reactions became so severe that she developed panic attacks. The panic attacks developed into agoraphobia. She entered into treatment for allergies. According to Dr. Braly, her phobia abated and she was able to resume a normal life. I was somewhat skeptical of this and others of Dr. Braly's success stories until I talked to a close friend who had a very similar experience. The following provides you with some information about her.

Case Study: Jordi and I were having a conversation about various phases in her life in which she had engaged in extreme sports and activities fearlessly. All of Jordi's friends admired her for this adventurous spirit. One day Jordi felt "odd." This odd sensation expanded to severe disorientation, shakiness, dizziness, tunnel-vision and a feeling of dissociation from her surroundings. These feelings were accompanied by fear, which soon expanded into panic episodes. Her physician diagnosed her as having a panic disorder and immediately prescribed medication. Jordi felt strongly that medication was not a reasonable solution until she had exhausted other avenues of treatment. Eventually she found her way to an orthomolecular psychiatrist—a specialist in finding the nutritional imbalances responsible for creating symptoms of mental illness.

The orthomolecular psychiatrist diagnosed her condition as acute hypoglycemia. Her treatment consisted of some alteration in her diet, particularly in the frequency of her meals and snacks. Regardless of whether or not she felt hungry, she was advised to eat protein every 3 to 4 hours.

She now exercises regularly, avoids sugar and takes vitamin and mineral supplements. The panic episodes never returned. When Jordi occasionally forgets to eat, she does notice that the symptoms start to reappear. Upon her recognition of these symptoms, she will simply eat some protein. The symptoms abate almost immediately. Jordi's experience is not unusual. Fortunately she found the right help before she developed a more

serious symptomology.   Had Jordi taken the medication prescribed by the first doctor, chances are that she would have
accepted her panic disorder as permanent and remained on
medication indefinitely.

The material in this chapter was designed to provide you
with enough information to select the form of treatment that
best suits your particular situation.   You should keep in mind
that an extensive medical evaluation is essential before you
explore alternative health care.   You may also want to discuss
this with your physician.

It is also critical that you understand that these treatment
options should not be used to the exclusion of psychotherapy.
If all of your physical symptoms magically disappeared tomorrow,
you still may have learned avoidance behaviors—these will not
go away on their own.   Using the techniques in this book and,
if possible, seeking out therapy with a specialist, is critical to
your recovery.

Chapter 8

WHEN MEDICATION IS NECESSARY

Whether or not to take medication for anxiety is probably the question most frequently asked by my patients. Some have been on a variety of medications for years with only modest results. Others have been too afraid to consider taking medication despite the urging of physicians and psychiatrists. Patients have varied backgrounds. Each needs to be evaluated individually.

Before you make a decision about medication, you should be as informed as possible. You need to know about the types of medications available, their indications, their contraindications and their side effects, as well as their effectiveness and dosages. I have provided that information for you with one caveat. You should, under no circumstances, take a drug without direct supervision by your doctor. The information provided is to be used when considering medication from your physician or psychiatrist. If this decision is to be made in concert with another practitioner as well, the person should be a licensed health care professional.

When we take a closer look at whether or not medication is indicated, it is helpful to understand more about the types of medications frequently prescribed. For example, antianxiety medication can be prescribed for both agoraphobia as well as for fear of public speaking. However, if the individual shows signs of anxiety only when speaking in public, then, rather than an antianxiety medication, a beta blocker such as Inderal may be indicated. Or, if someone has free-floating anxiety and depression but does not have panic attacks or agoraphobia, an antidepressant medication may be more appropriate than an antianxiety medication such as Xanax. Confusing? Well, medications certainly are complex, which is why the prescribing of medication is always left up to a physician or a psychiatrist.

However, as I have mentioned earlier, it is helpful to have an additional framework within which to make your decisions. The most common medications used for treating anxiety will be carefully outlined for your review in the next few pages. The medications are broken down into the categories of minor tranquilizers, benzodiazepines, barbiturates, beta-adrenergic blocking drugs (beta blockers), antidepressant drugs (both bicyclic and tricyclic), hypnotic sedatives and anticonvulsant drugs.

Each of these drug classes have a brand name and a chemical name. The brand names will appear in bold. The chemical names will appear in italics.

MINOR TRANQUILIZERS

Buspirone (BuSpar)

This drug was initially developed as a medication for persons with psychosis but it failed to live up to its expectations, having very little impact on psychosis. It was observed to have a significant effect on symptoms of aggression and agitation. This was very exciting, especially at first. The drug had demonstrated a potential for treating anxiety without the use of tranquilizers known as benzodiazepines. BuSpar is classified as a non-sedating anxiolytic medication. It is a partial agonist at serotonin reuptake sites, modulating the neurotransmitters in the mid brain.

When it was initially prescribed in the late 1980's, anxiety experts were very optimistic. Unfortunately, it has now shown to be less effective for combating symptoms of panic disorder. BuSpar has had its best results with generalized anxiety disorder and has been shown to decrease symptoms of OCD. The side effects of BuSpar include nausea, tachycardia, dizziness and depression. In higher dosages it may cause tremors, alterations of menstruation and sexual dysfunction. Taking this drug requires no limitation on types of foods, beverages, alcohol, tobacco, or activities enjoyed by the patient.

Hydroxyzine (Atarax Vistaril)
This minor tranquilizer is in reality an antihistamine used to treat anxiety. It is rarely effective for panic disorder but has no side effects other than dry mouth and fatigue.

Meprobamate (Equanil or Miltown)
Meprobamate came on the market in the mid-1950's and was promoted as a muscle relaxant or sedative. It is often prescribed as an antianxiety drug. However, some experts believe that it may be more addictive than Valium or other benzodiazepines. One advantage is that for individuals who experience paradoxical reactions to benzodiazepines, this drug is often better tolerated in addition to being less expensive. (Paradoxical reactions mean that instead of relaxing the patient, a drug can have a reverse effect, causing him/her to become more agitated.) Side effects include seizures in epileptics, dependence, over-sedation, and malcoordination.

ANTI-CONVULSANT DRUGS

AntiEpileptic Drugs
Carbamazepine (Tegretol)
This drug was introduced in the mid-1950's for the treatment of epilepsy. In the 1970's, it was discovered to be effective in managing some of the manic symptoms caused by manic-depressive illness. This drug is therefore referenced as a "mood stabilizer," although it is an anti-convulsant. Although

some anti-convulsants are currently used to treat anxiety, a mood stabilizer is primarily reserved for mood disorders such as bipolar illness or manic depression. Carbamazepine or Tegretol has been prescribed on occasion to treat extreme cases of anxiety when other drugs have failed. Sometimes Tegretol is used in combination with lithium or certain antidepressant medications. Side effects from this medication can be serious. Aplastic anemia can occur in addition to certain adverse reactions, although these reactions are rare, occurring only in about one case in ten thousand. For the first six months, it is often recommended that blood counts be taken on a weekly basis. More than likely this type of drug will not be prescribed for your symptoms of anxiety. If it is, you may want to discuss the side effects and dosages thoroughly with your physician or psychiatrist.

Clonazapam (Klonopin)

Klonopin is an anti-convulsant benzodiazepine. It was originally used for the treatment of epilepsy. More recently, it has been used for its anti-panic effect. For some individuals who have previously been unresponsive to benzodiazepines such as Valium, Xanax and Ativan, Klonopin has developed quite a reputation for managing even the most difficult cases of anxiety. Klonopin is often prescribed in conjunction with antidepressant medications to combat anxiety and/or depression. While Klonopin is evolving into the drug of choice where benzodiazepines are concerned, it does have the potential for certain side effects. Like most, Klonopin can cause poor muscle control, dizziness, and drowsiness in either depressed or elevated moods. Less common side effects include the following: bed-wetting, liver inflammation, coated tongue, abnormal eye movements, inability to express thoughts, double vision, coma, headaches, temporary paralysis, tremors, labored breathing, shortness of breath, fainting, confusion, forgetfulness, hallucinations, suicidal acts, hair loss, heart palpitations, appetite changes, etc. Other symptoms include: fever, swollen lymph glands, stomach irritation.

But these are only "potential" side effects. These are not very common and most often will not occur when the drug is taken in the dosages prescribed for anxiety which are different from the dosages prescribed for epilepsy. However, withdrawal symptoms can be very dangerous if the withdrawal is done improperly. Be certain to use this drug under the careful supervision of your doctor.

BENZODIAZEPINES

Benzodiazepines can be broken down into 1) hypnotic sedatives 2) anti-convulsants and 3) general benzodiazepines. Benzodiazepines affect the receptor sides of certain areas of the brain, producing a substance called GABA (gamma-amino butyric acid). Certain types of benzodiazepines will determine whether the effect on these receptors will be primarily that of an anti-convulsant sedative or of an anti-panic drug. For example, Quantatin is used both as an anti-convulsant and an antianxiety drug. It is part of the benzodiazepine family, yet acts very differently than the benzodiazepines that are designed for sleep or relaxation. The benzodiazepines designed to help with relaxation are the following:

Hypnotic Benzodiazepines
Flurazepam (Dalmane)
Dalmane is a sedative or sleeping medicine. This drug is prescribed for people with insomnia. It is a member of the group related to benzodiazepines. Dalmane is also used as an antianxiety agent and sedative. These drugs create the relaxation a person needs to fall asleep. Caution in taking this drug is necessary because of the potential for abuse. Symptoms of withdrawal can include convulsions, tremors, stomach and muscle cramps, insomnia, agitation, vomiting, diarrhea and sweating.

Do not take this medication if you are allergic to it or to similar drugs such as Ativan, Valium, or Klonopin. Do not take

Dalmane within three months of pregnancy unless under the strict supervision of your doctor. Dalmane does have the capacity to cause a hangover the next day. Taking it on a daily basis can cause problems.

Quazepam (Dural)

Quazepam is a type of sedative or hypnotic prescribed for insomnia and anxiety. This drug works by relaxing the large muscles throughout the body and by increasing the effect of GABA. GABA is an amino acid (an organic compound whose chief component is protein) located in the brain which slows down nerve transmission. Quazepam has the characterization of Valium. These drugs are used as sleeping pills, anti-convulsants and anxiety agents. More daytime drowsiness is experienced by someone using Quazepam than with other sedatives. After a period of time, excessive tolerance to the drug may arise in some people. This happens because the body's makeup has a mechanism that tries to get the drug out of the blood as soon as possible. If this drug is abruptly discontinued, withdrawal symptoms may include convulsions, tremors, muscle cramps, insomnia, agitation, diarrhea, vomiting and sweating. Do not take this drug if you are allergic to drugs that are similar. This drug may cause birth defects. Or, a child may be born dependent on the medication.

Anti-Panic Benzodiazepines
Diazepam (Valium)

Valium is a central nervous system depressant. It absorbs rapidly when taken by mouth and has a long half life, which means it remains in the system for a long time, in contrast to other benzodiazepines. One five milligram dose can last all day, although the recommended dosage for anxiety can be anywhere from five milligrams to forty milligrams per day.

Valium was frequently over-prescribed in the 1960's. This left many patients physically and psychologically dependent on the drug. Consequently, many psychiatrists and physicians are reluctant to prescribe Valium as part of a regular antianxiety regime. Valium is becoming increasingly unpopular, its role is being replaced by newer benzodiazepines such as Ativan and Xanax.

Valium remains for some patients an effective antianxiety medication. For others, it seems too sedating and not nearly as effective as some of the more popular antianxiety agents. The more common side effects of Valium can include drowsiness, slurred speech, and malcoordination. Less common side effects are constipation, dry mouth, dizziness, tremor, incontinence, difficulty falling asleep, liver dysfunction and withdrawal symptoms.

Alprazolam (Xanax)

Xanax is classified as a benzodiazepine. It is approved for managing anxiety.

When Xanax was initially introduced in the 1970's, physicians and psychiatrists were extremely excited because clinical trials seemed to indicate that the drug was not "addictive." Therefore, Xanax was prescribed liberally for all sorts of problems, from sleep to anxiety to depression. Several years later, the truth was revealed about Xanax. Although in many cases it proved superior to Valium in its ability to alleviate anxiety, its potential for withdrawal symptoms have proven to be similar to that of Valium. Many physicians discovered that their patients became addicted to Xanax. Although Xanax can be as much of a potential threat as Valium in terms of withdrawal reactions, most doctors are still reluctant to prescribe Valium. They maintain that Xanax is safer.

Lorazepam (Ativan)

Lorazepam is a benzodiazepine like Valium but is considered to be milder because its effects are not long-lasting. Ativan can be very effective in managing anxiety symptoms without causing the individual to feel too drugged. If taken at bedtime, it has almost no hangover effect—it leaves the system very rapidly. In medical terms, it has a short half-life. Ativan is absorbed in the intestine, which means that its effects can be influenced by how much food is in your stomach. If you plan to take Ativan for a specific situation in which you anticipate feeling anxious, you may want to make sure your stomach is empty or it may take a little longer to work. Withdrawal symptoms may occur if a prolonged use of the drug is halted abruptly. Other side effects include memory loss (particularly in older persons), labored breathing, tiredness, drowsiness and confusion. The average dose is from 2 to 6 milligrams per day.

ANTIDEPRESSANTS

Imipramine (Tofranil)

This drug is used to abate or manage bed-wetting, pain, cocaine withdrawal symptoms, attention deficit disorder, binging and purging, and panic attacks and agoraphobia. As is the case with most antidepressants, the mechanism that causes this drug to work has not been clearly established. For depression and anxiety, it is thought that this drug, like other depressants, affects the serotonin in the brain. This drug is the "drug of choice" for agoraphobia. The usual adult dosage for anxiety or depression is around seventy-five milligrams per day orally. This is usually divided into three doses, which may be increased slowly every week to see at what point the drug begins to become effective and tolerated.

Fluoxetine (Prozac)

Prozac is an antidepressant that is prescribed to patients with common depression. It is unrelated to the older tricyclic and tetracyclic antidepressants. It blocks the reuptake of serotonin into the nervous system cells. Prozac helps to improve mood, mental alertness, physical activity and sleep patterns. Some people experience weight loss on this drug, especially in underweight depressed people. Those people with severe liver or kidney damage should take Prozac at lower dosages than normal. The most common side effects of fluoxetine involve anxiety, nervousness, sleeplessness, drowsiness, weakness, tremors, sweating, dry mouth, upset stomach, appetite loss, nausea, rash, itching, vomiting and diarrhea. Fifteen percent of those initially taking this drug in one study stopped because of its side effects.[5]

Prozac may prolong the effects of Diazepam and other benzodiazepine type drugs in your body. Little is actually known about taking Prozac in combination with other nervous system agents. At least two weeks should fall between taking a monoamine oxidase inhibitor (MAO) and Prozac. Usually twenty to forty milligrams a day are taken, but in some cases, eighty milligrams per day. People have occasionally died of Prozac overdoses, but they are rare. Symptoms of overdosage include seizures, vomiting, nausea, agitation, restlessness and nervous system excitation. If an overdose occurs, always bring the bottle with you for examination by attending medical personnel.

Bupropin (**Wellbutrin**)

Bupropin is a unicyclic drug. It was released in 1989. It had been planned for release in 1986, but there were some extended studies made, because of an outbreak of seizures in bulimic patients, to determine the probability of seizures in depressed patients. Bupropin does not inhibit monoamine oxidase. It is not a norepinephrine or a serotonin reuptaker blocker like Prozac. In animals at high dosages and blood levels, however, Bupropin effectively acts as a blockade. This drug is effective in depression and in some treatment of resistant panic disorder patients. It takes full effect in three to four weeks. Anyone with a history of seizures, heart attacks and heart disease should be extra careful while taking this medication. This drug has caused liver damage in animals and should be taken with caution by someone with a history of liver disease. Breast-feeding women should not take Bupropin because it can be passed to their child. Older adults haven't had any reported problems. Side effects of this drug include dry mouth, sleeplessness, headaches, nausea, vomiting, constipation and tremors. One out of ten people who begin taking this drug must quit because of intolerable side effects. Bupropin may increase the breakdown of carbamazepine, cremetidine, and then phenobarbital, or pthenytoin. Those people taking these medications simultaneously should increase their dosage of Bupropin. Any drug used along with Bupropin that increases the chance of a seizure should be monitored or avoided.

Trazodone (Desyrel)

Desyrel is usually prescribed for someone with depression without anxiety. Also, it is prescribed for individuals in treatment for cocaine withdrawal and aggressive behaviors. This drug is different from other antidepressants and is less likely to cause side effects. For those taking Desyrel, a change can be detected in as little as two weeks from the day that the medication has started. Four weeks is required before any greater difference is noticeable. It is recommended that people who have recently undergone a heart attack wait some time before taking this medication. Those with a history of heart problems should avoid this drug altogether. Pregnant women and breast feeders should not take this drug. Side effects include upset stomach, constipation, abdominal pains, bad taste in mouth, nausea, diarrhea, palpitations, irregular heartbeat, rashes, swelling, large increases or decreases in blood pressure, and difficulty breathing, to name a few. This drug is best taken with food in order to absorb into the bloodstream and reduce possible stomach upset, dizziness or weakness. The dosage is usually about one hundred and fifty milligrams a day to start. Thereafter, on the third and fourth day, an increase of fifty milligrams is prescribed until a peak of four hundred milligrams a day has been reached. Try to avoid alcohol when under the influence of this drug.

Fluvoxamine (Luvox)

Luvox was introduced in 1995 as a selective serotonin reuptake inhibitor. It is prescribed for panic, generalized anxiety and depression but has enjoyed its greatest success with obsessive-compulsive disorder. It may also have a role in helping to manage eating disorders and headaches. Dosages range from fifty milligrams to three hundred milligrams.

Side effects can include nausea, vomiting, impaired sexual function, liver toxicity (rare), headaches, agitation, tremors, dry mouth. This drug should not be taken with the medications seldane or hismanal.

Paroxetine (Paxil)

Paxil has been approved by the FDA for the treatment of obsessive-compulsive disorder and panic disorder. Paxil also inhibits serotonin in the brain and is reported to have fewer side effects than tricyclic antidepressants. Dosages range from ten milligrams to fifty milligrams.

Side effects may include loss of appetite, tingling of hands, dizziness upon standing (orthostatic hypotension), headaches, blurred vision, palpitations, nervousness, and motion sickness. Paxil has been reported to cause withdrawal symptoms upon abrupt cessation. Symptoms of withdrawal may include motion sickness, dizziness, confusion.

Sertraline (Zoloft)

Zoloft has been approved by the FDA for the treatment of depression. Its effectiveness on panic attacks has been disappointing although it does appear to have some benefit for symptoms of obsessive-compulsive disorder. It is also one of the SSRI classification of antidepressants which are reported to have less side effects than tricyclics. Dosages range from fifty milligrams to two hundred milligrams. Zoloft is reported to be less likely to cause weight gain or orthostatic hypotension (dip in blood pressure upon rising), urinary retention. Side effects may include rash, dizziness, anemia, blurred vision, confusion. This drug may impair sexual function in males and females.

Nefazodone (Serzone)

Serzone, introduced in 1994, is a 5-H2 antagonist and is one of the more recent medications available. It is reported to have fewer side effects than many of the previously mentioned medications. It is widely prescribed for depression and may have a role in pain management. It has not shown to be particularly effective in combating symptoms of panic attacks or generalized anxiety. Dosages range from one hundred milligrams to six hundred milligrams. Side effects may include skin rash, dry mouth, blurred vision, insomnia, headaches, dizziness, agitation and anxiety, lowered blood pressure, impaired sexual function, particularly in males.

Clomipramine (Anafranil)

Anafranil was introduced in 1970 as a treatment for severe depression and obsessive-compulsive disorder. Anafranil has also proven to be effective in the treatment of generalized anxiety disorder and panic attacks. Anafranil is a tricyclic antidepressant. Dosages range from fifty milligrams to two hundred fifty milligrams. Side effects may include sedation, drug fever, increased appetite, weight gain, headache, memory impairment, nausea, vomiting, confusion, disorientation, depression, and muscle cramps.

Venlafaxine (Effexor)

Effexor was introduced in 1993 as a bycyclic antidepressant. It is FDA Approved for the treatment of depression although Effexor has indications for obsessive-compulsive disorder. It has not been clinically proven to be effective for panic or generalized anxiety. Dosages range from seventy-five milligrams to two hundred and twenty-five milligrams. Side effects include anxiety, increased blood pressure, seizures (rare), increased heart rate, nausea, vomiting, weight loss. This drug may also cause impaired sexual function in both males and females. Effexor should not be taken concurrently with Tagamet.

All antidepressant medications have the potential to affect liver and kidney functioning. If taken for over three months, periodic monitoring should be done by your doctor. This is particularly true of individuals sixty years of age and older. Additionally, many of the medications do not react well with other drugs, particularly MAOI's and, in some cases, acid blockers. Before taking any medication over-the-counter or prescribed, check with your physician first. Additionally, restrict alcohol use with all tranquilizers and antidepressants.

MONOAMINE OXIDASE INHIBITORS (MAOI's)

It is not necessary to know exactly how MAOI's work except to know that they involve certain enzymes and the inhibition of monoamine oxidase. These drugs have been used not only for depression but also in patients with Parkinson's disease. There are fore kinds of MAOI's. The following MAOI's are listed along with their brand names, typical dosage in milligrams, and their side effects.

The most common side effects are the reactions with food. There are specific foods that must not be eaten because they interfere with the effectiveness of the MAOI's and can be very dangerous. Side effects of high blood pressure and a subsequent hypertensive crisis, orthostatic hypotension (a drop in blood pressure upon standing produces dizziness) are all potential side effects. Other side effects include dry mouth, dizziness, weight gain, sexual impotency, muscle cramps, insomnia. The most serious side effects occur as the result of food and drug interactions. The following table lists the types of foods and drugs that would be contraindicated while using MAOI's:

FOOD	DRUGS
Beer and red wine	Demerol
Aged cheeses	Epinephrine
Smoked fish	Ephedrine
Liver	Cold remedies
Brewer's yeast	Local anesthetics
Green beans	
Sausage	

When MAOI's break down in the body, a substance called Tyramine is produced. The foods and medications listed contain Tyramine, and an abundance of this chemical can cause a rise in blood pressure. If you are taking MAOI's, check with your physician regarding restrictions on any medication and always review warnings about drug interactions before purchasing any over-the-counter drug.

Selegiline (Eldepryl)

Selegiline was initially used for the treatment of depression at high dosages of fifteen to sixty milligrams per day. Recently, under the official trade name Eldepryl, the drug has been helpful in the treatment of Parkinson's disease at lower dosages of five to ten milligrams per day. It appears that this drug is the safest of the older MAOI's and has fewer side effects. The older MAOI antidepressants work in both the MAOI A and B forms and affect the entire body, whereas Selegiline is found only in the brain, causing the increased or longer-lasting activity of dopamine in the brain. How this happens, we are unsure. Individuals on this drug must follow a strict diet. The pills are considered to be expensive. But at least the drug doesn't cause sexual dysfunction, anxiety or insomnia. Other common side effects are headaches, nausea, vomiting, light-headedness, abdominal pains, uncontrolled muscle spasms, high blood pressure, anxiety, changes in moods, erratic sleep patterns, aches and pains, and increased energy. The drug may hasten tooth decay, cavities, and infections in the mouth due to dry mouth. Drug interactions: Selegiline should not be taken with Meprodine or other narcotics. It may be fatal or severe. Alcohol in combination with the drug may cause headaches, high blood pressure, fever. Take it with food or meals to avoid nausea.

Other MAOI's

Isocarboxazid (Marplan)—therapeutic dosage is thirty to fifty milligrams per day.

Phenelzine (Nardil)—therapeutic dosage is forty-five to ninety milligrams per day.

Tranylcypromine (Parnate)—therapeutic dosage is thirty to fifty milligrams per day.

BETA BLOCKERS

Noradrenergic (Agents)

Beta blockers were originally prescribed for heart problems and migraine headaches. Investigations of stage performers later revealed that beta blockers ameliorated the physical symptoms often associated with anxiety (heart palpitations, sweating, disorientation, tremors). Beta blockers are most often prescribed for stage fright. They are commonly used by comedians, actors, and musicians as a means of reducing performance anxiety without causing drowsiness (the pitfall of using benzodiazepines). Individuals who suffer from situational anxiety can benefit greatly from this drug. Panic disorder and GAD sufferers may not enjoy the same benefits.

Beta blockers are sometimes used as a stopgap measure to help minimize symptoms of withdrawal from benzodiazepines. Once withdrawal is successful, the beta blockers are usually discontinued. they have their own side effects which should be considered in their long-term use. The beta blockers most frequently prescribed for performance anxiety or social phobia are propranolol, oxprenolol, pindolol, atenolol, and clonidine. The side effects from these drugs include low blood pressure, headaches, disorientation or light-headedness, gastrointestinal upset, agitation or anxiety (particularly in anxiety patients), possible bronchospasms in asthmatic patients, dry mouth, and fatigue.

CONCLUSION

Did you know that more people seek treatment from their physicians for symptoms of anxiety than for symptoms of the common cold? Whether a particular person's anxiety derives from a panic disorder, GAD, PTSD, or an adjustment disorder, anxiety has reached epidemic proportions. Anyone who has experienced anxiety on a consistent basis can attest to the far-reaching effects it can have. In writing this book, I remembered the terror and hopelessness I felt each time an attack would occur. I recalled all of those mornings that I attempted to leave the house and, after closing the door behind me, was consumed by panic so severe that I had to turn around and go home. I believed at that time that no one would ever be able to help me. So I lived a life of isolation and despair. I hit bottom and was ready to do one of two things, get better or die. I knew I could no longer exist in a vacuum, watching the goals I had worked so hard to achieve begin to slip slowly out of my grasp. I cried and cried until I got angry. As the anger welled up inside, I realized I wasn't as fragile as I had believed. I would not allow this disease to overpower me any longer. From that day on, I learned that, although anxiety is uncomfortable, it is not powerful enough to make me go crazy or kill me. I also learned that there is such a thing as appropriate anxiety. Last year, while on an airplane, I noticed my stomach felt a little funny. I was able to identify that I was nervous. As I looked around me, I noticed many passengers ordering cocktails, seeming to coincide with the sudden onset of turbulence. I realized that experiencing some degree of anxiety during a particularly turbulent flight is an appropriate response. Circumstances that either feel potentially life-threatening or threatening to our sense of self can generate an anxious reaction.

Recognizing the place anxiety has in our lives is essential. Without anxiety, we would be emotionally anesthetized. For example, if you were to make an important speech and did not feel apprehensive, then perhaps you would not really care about whether or not you made an impact on your audience. Or, if you were to go on a date for the first time with someone to whom you were very attracted, and felt totally calm, it could indicate you had no feelings about the impression you made. Our reactions are a reflection of our emotional investment, which inevitably translates into a certain amount of anxiety and excitement. The difficulty rises out of being unable to recognize the role anxiety plays in our lives and to allow it to exist without buying into the myth that it has to be out of control.

If you have read this book thoroughly, it is time to assimilate and utilize the information that you have worked so hard to understand. Your commitment to recovery is what has inspired you into picking up this book in the first place. Harness that commitment into a healthy, righteous anger; not at yourself, but at your anxiety. The fear is only as large and as ugly as you allow it to be. Get tough, get determined, and most of all, get going! Now is the time to take charge of your life.

ENDNOTES

[1]Harold Levinson with Steven Carter, *Phobia Free* (M. Evans and Company, Inc., 1986), p.53.

[2]William G. Crook, M.D., *The Yeast Connection* (Professional Books, 1983, 1984), p.1.

[3]Written by a former patient of Open Doors Institute.

[4]James Braly, M.D., *Food Allergy & Nutrition* (Keats Publishing, 1992).

[5]Bert Stern, Lawrence D. Chelnick, Harold M. Silverman, Gilbert Simon, *The Pill Book* ScP (Bantam Books, 1992), 5th ed.

RESOURCES

NEWSLETTERS

The National Panic/Anxiety Disorder Newsletter, 1718 Burgandy Place, Suite B, Santa Rosa, CA, (707) 5275738.

Encourage Newsletter, 13610 North Scottsdale Rd., Suite 10-126, Scottsdale, AZ 85254.

SUPPORT GROUPS

Crohn's and Colitis Foundation of America, 444 Park Ave. So., New York, NY 10008, (800) 932-2423

Los Angeles Gay and Lesbian Center - Same Gender Domestic Violence Program, (213) 933-7640.

National Domestic Violence Hotline, (800) 799-7233

Phobic Anonymous World Service Headquarters, P.O. Box 1180, Palm Springs, CA 92263, (619) 322-COPE. (12-step self-help support group for agoraphobics)

TREATMENT FACILITIES, REFERENCE NUMBERS

Suicide Prevention, 1-800-333-4444.

Crises Intervention, 1-800-833-3376.

Open Doors Institute, (818) 710-6442. 13601 Ventura Boulevard, Suite 600, Sherman Oaks, CA 91423; website: http://www.opendoorsinstitute.com. Treatment for Anxiety and Depression, utilizing a network of providers. (Phone sessions available)

Anxiety Disorders Association of America, 11900 Parklawn Dr. Suite 100, Rockville, MD, (301) 231-9350 http://www.adaa.org

National Depression and Manic-Depressive Association, 730 N. Franklin St., Suite 501, Chicago, IL 60610, (800) 82NDMDA.

Report from Center for Mental Health Services ADA Roundtable January 25-26 1995 - Copies of report are available from: National Mental Health Services Knowledge Exchange Network, P.O. Box 42490, Washington, D.C. 20015, (800) 789-2647 / (301) 443-9006 TDD

National Paruresis Association 1-800-247-3864 P.O. Box 26225, Baltimore, MD 21210

BIBLIOGRAPHY

CHAPTER 1

Arch. Gen. Psychiatry, *Increased Sensitivity to Caffeine in Patients With Panic Disorder.* Vol. 41, November 1984.

Aronson, Thomas A., M.D. and Craig, Thomas J., M.D., *M.P.L.* (Am. J. Psychiatry 143: 643-645, 1986).

Becker, Ernest, *Denial of Death.* Free Press, London: 1983, pg. 208.

Bowlby, J.: *Separation Anxiety and Anger.* New York, Basic Books, 1978.

Cohen, M.E. High Familial Prevalence of Circulatory Asthenia. *Am. J. Hum. Genet.* 1951; 3:126-128.

Crook, William G., M.D., *The Yeast Connection,* Professional Books, 1983, 1984, pg. 1.

Crowe, R.C., Pauls, D.L., Slymen, D.J. et al: *A Family Study of Anxiety Neurosis;* Morbidity risk in families of patients with and without mitral valve prolapse. Arch. Gen. Psychiatry.

Crowe, R.R., Noyes, R., Jr., Pauls, D.L. et al; *A Family Study of Panic Disorder.* Arch. Gen. Psychiatry 1983; 40-1065-1069.

DSM IV (4th edition). American Psychiatric Association, Washington, D.C., 1994.

Frankenhaeuser, M., Jarpe, G. Psychophysiological Reactions to Infusions of a Mixture of Adrenalin and Noradrenalin. Scand. J. Psychol. 1962: 3:21-28.

(Golub 1976; Alplanals et al 1977; Lahmeyor et al 1982; Veith et al 1984; Van Den Akker and Steptoe 1985).

Gorman, J.K., Fyer, A.J., Gliklich, J., King, D., Klein, D.F.: Mitral Valve Prolapse and Panic Disorder: *Anxiety New Research and Changing Concepts.* New York, Raven Press 1981.

Gorman, J.M., Martinez, J.M., Liebowitz, M.D. et al: *Hypoglycemia and Panic Attacks.* Am. J. Psychiatry, 1984: 141:101-102.

Kelly, D.H., Mi: Measurement of Anxiety by Forearm Blood Flow. *Br. J. Psychiatry* 1971; 119-129-141.

Klein, D.F.; Anxiety reconceptualized in Klein, D.F., Rabkin, S.G. (eds) Anxiety - New Research and Changing Concepts. New York, Raven Press 1981.

Levinson, Harold with Carter, Steven, *Phobia Free.* M. Evans and Company, Inc., 1986, pg. 53.

Marks, I. Lader: Anxiety States (Anxiety Neurosis): A Review of *J. Nerv. Dis* 1973; 156-3-18.

Morrison, James: *When Psychological Problems Mask Medical Disorders,* Guilford Press, New York, New York, 1997.

Pitts, F.N., Jr., Allen, R.E.: Biochemical Induction of Anxiety in Fann W.E., Karacan I., Pokorny, A.D., Williams, R.L. (eds) *Phenomonology and Treatment of Anxiety,* New York, S.P. Medical & Scientific Books.

Pitts F.N., Jr., McClure, J.N., Jr.: Lactate Metabolism in Anxiety Neurosis. *N. Engl. J. Med.* 1967: 2227:1329-1336.

Roth, W.T., Ticklenberg, J.R., Doyle, C.M. et al; Mood States and 24-Hour Cardiac Monitoring. *J. Phychosom Res.* 1976; 20:179-186.

Schwartz, Jeffery: *Brain Lock - Free Yourself from Obsessive-Compulsive Behavior.* 1996 Regan Books, New York

Slater, E., Shields, J.: Genetic Aspects of Anxiety in Lader M.H. (ed) *Studies of Anxiety,* London, Hecity Brothers. 1968; 140-237-236.

Van Den Hout, Marcel A.; Gniez, Erk. *Brit. J. Psychiatry,* 1984; 144, 503-507.

Van Dis H; Hyperventilation in Phobic Patients in Spielberger C.D., Sarason, I.G. (eds) *Stress and Anxiety* New York, Halsted Press 1978 Vol. 5.

Weeks, Claire, *Peace From Nervous Suffering*, Hawthorne Books, Inc., N.Y.: 1972, pg. 42.

Wilson, R. Reid, Ph.D., Paul Goodman, Ph.D., *Don't Panic, Taking Control of Anxiety Attacks*, Julian Press, 1951.

CHAPTER 2

Berry, Dawn Bradly: *The Domestic Violence Sourcebook*, RGA Publishing Group, California, 1995 and 1996.

Boulenger, Jean-Philippe, M.D., Uhde, Thomas W., M.D., Wolffe, Edward A., III, and Post, Robert M., M.D., *Increased Sensitivity to Caffeine in Patients with Panic Disorder.*   Arch. Gen. Psychiatry - Vol 41, Nov. 1984.

Hudson, Charles J., M.D., Sherrod H. Perkins, M.A., E.A.C., et al.,   *Panic Disorder & Alcohol Misuse*, Journal of Studies on Alcohol, Vol. 45, Nov. 5, 1984.

Merck Manual, Merck Research Laboratories, New Jersey, 16th Ed., 5th printing, 1996.

Renzetti, Claire, Miley, Charles Harvey, Editors: *Violence in Gay and Lesbian Domestic Partnerships*, 1996, Park Press, Harrington Park Press, Binghampton, New York.

Salber, Patricia R., M.D., Ferro, Ellen Talia, M.D.: *The Physicians Guide to Domestic Violence/How to Ask the Right Questions and Recognize Abuse*, Volcano Press, California, 1995.

CHAPTER 4

Barnhart, Edward, *Physicians Desk Reference.* Medical Economics Co., 1997.

Braly, James, M.D., *Food Allergy & Nutrition.* Keats Publishing, 1992.

DSM IV (4th edition). American Psychiatric Association, Washington, D.C., 1994.

Merck Manual, Merck Research Laboratories, New Jersey, 5th printing, 1996.

Nambudripad, Devi, D.C., Ph.D., *You Can Reprogram Your Brain to Perfect Health.* Singer Publishing, 1989.

Werbach, Melvyn, M.D., *Nutritional Influences on Illness - A Sourcebook of Clinical Research,* 3rd Line Press, 1988.

CHAPTER 5

Beck, Aaron T., Rush, A. John, Shaw, Brian F., Emery, Gary, *Cognitive Therapy of Depression,* Guilfold Press, New York, 1979.

Burns, David D., *Feeling Good, the New Mood Therapy,* Avon Books, New York, 1980.

Seligman, Martin E. and Meyer, Steven S., *Failure to Escape Traumatic Shock,* Journal of Experimental Psychology, Vol. 74, No. 1, p. 1-9, 1967.

CHAPTER 7

Bloomfield, Harold H., M.D., Nordhrs, Michael, M.D., McWilliams, Peter: *Hypericum and Depression,* Prelude Press, Santa Monica, California, 1996.

Burton Golden Group, *Alternative Medicine - The Definitive Guide,* Future Medicine Publishing, Poughkeepsie, New York, 1994.

Weil, Andrew, M.D.: *Spontaneous Healing,* Alford A. Knopf, Inc., New York, 1995

CHAPTER 8

Barnhart, Edward, *Physicians Desk Reference.* Medical Economics Co., 1997 version.

Hong, James A., M.D., *The Essential Guide to Prescription Drugs,* Harper Perennial, New York, 1997.

Schatzberg, Alan S., M.D., and Cole, Jonathan O., M.D., *Manual of Clinical Psychopharmacology,* New Ed., American Psychiatric Press, Inc., Washington, D.C., 1997.

Stern, Bert; Chelnick, Lawrence D.; Silverman, Harold M.; Simon, Gilbert; *The Pill Book,* Bantam Books, 5th Ed., 1992.

GLOSSARY OF TERMS

AAA - Refers to the cognitive formula, **Ask • Answer • Alternatives**, used to combat symptoms of Generalized Anxiety Disorder and depression.

Adjustment Disorder - Refers to anxiety and/or depression erupting in response to specific life changes. The symptoms often abate once the individual is no longer in transition.

Agoraphobia - An anxiety disorder which causes one to be afraid of leaving home or familiar surroundings. Agoraphobia may accompany panic attacks, or exist as the result of limited symptom attacks such as vomiting and diarrhea.

Anger as Power - A psychotherapeutic technique referring to the externalization of anxiety represented by an ominous creature. The creature, previously perceived as threatening, is confronted with the individual's anger in combination with Animation Visualization. The anger serves to quash the anxiety, facilitating the diminution of anxiety symptoms, and engender a feeling of success.

Animation Visualization - An antianxiety tool utilizing cartoon-like imagery to disempower and demystify anxiety. This technique is used in conjunction with Anger as Power.

Anorexia - Anorexia Nervosa is an eating disorder which usually develops in adolescent females. Due to a distorted body image, the individual deliberately denies the body sustenance, causing abnormal weight loss and sometimes death.

Antidepressants - Medications which affect neurotransmitters associated with anxiety and depression. These drugs include Selective Serotonin Reuptake Inhibitors (SSRIs) and first and second generational tricyclics. These drugs are not addictive, although certain reactions may occur upon cessation.

Anxiety - A psychological and physiological state in which trepidation is experienced as the result of specific "cues". These cues vary depending upon whether or not a particular anxiety disorder is present. Anxiety may be free-floating or culminate into acute episodes.

Benzodiazepines - A classification of drugs used to combat symptoms of anxiety and insomnia through depression of the central nervous system. These medications include: Xanax, Ativan, Valium, Klonopin and others. Because of the potential for abuse and addiction, these drugs are often prescribed for limited periods of time and require slow tapering to avoid symptoms of withdrawal.

Candida - A type of yeast that infects the body when the biochemistry is compromised due to drugs or illness. Candida most often affects the intestines, skin, vagina, and mouth, but can also enter the blood, causing systemic candida. These symptoms include disorientation, memory difficulties, rash, food allergies, and anxiety.

Cognitive Therapy - A style of psychotherapy premised on the theory that moods are determined by thoughts and not the other way around. This therapy punctuates control over symptoms through the isolation and reorganization of erroneous beliefs and expectations. This therapy is widely recognized for its success in treating both anxiety and depression.

Depression - A physiological and psychological state often attending anxiety. Symptoms include hopelessness, fatigue, isolation, helplessness, inability to concentrate, and sometimes suicidal feelings.

Detached Observer - A term used to describe the process by which one can dissociate from a panic attack. The individual psychically steps back and observes and views the severity of the fear as if it were happening to someone else.

GAD - Generalized Anxiety Disorder is an anxiety disorder characterized by an overconcern about health, job, or loved ones. Symptoms include excessive free-floating anxiety often accompanied by depression. The anxiety does not culminate into panic attacks. (Note: If panic attacks are present, an additional diagnosis of panic disorder may be indicated.)

Hyperthyroidism - A malady of the thyroid gland, causing an excessive amount of thyroid hormone to be produced. An overabundance of this chemical may create symptoms that mimic anxiety.

Hypoglycemia - A disorder of the endocrine system, causing the blood sugar level to dip below normal. This decrease in blood sugar may initiate symptoms of shakiness, disorientation, irritability, and anxiety.

Inner Ear Dysfunction - Refers to an impairment in the inner ear, causing symptoms of dizziness and disorientation, which may exacerbate symptoms of anxiety.

IST - Identify Stop and Transform is a cognitive formula used in treating anxiety. Anxiety-provoking thoughts are isolated and replaced with positive ones.

Mitral Valve Prolapse - An anomaly of the heart, impairing the function of the mitral valve. Symptoms include shortness of breath, fatigue and heart palpitations. M.V.P. is not dangerous but it can potentiate anxiety symptoms.

Obsessive-Compulsive Disorder - An anxiety disorder characterized by recurring unwanted thoughts and ritualistic behavior.

Panic Cycle - The model developed to represent various stages of experience when a panic disorder is present. The cycle proceeds as follows: 1) first panic attack, 2) anticipatory anxiety, 3) second panic attack, 4) avoidance, 5) relief, 6) sense of failure, 7) decision to confront object of fear, 8) anticipatory anxiety, 9) third panic attack, 10) avoidance. The stages revolve while the experience of anticipatory anxiety remains constant.

Panic Disorder - An anxiety disorder which includes symptoms of heart palpitations, sweating, disorientation, shortness of breath, and shaky limbs. These, along with other symptoms, manifest in dramatic episodes of acute anxiety so severe it may be interpreted as a heart attack or insanity.

Phobia - An irrational fear of a specific object, i.e. plants, birds, snakes, enclosed spaces.

ABOUT THE AUTHOR
Dr. Lynne Freeman

Over twenty-four million people in the United States suffer from some form of anxiety disorder. These figures are reported by the U.S. Department of Health. Anxiety disorders are today's most prevalent mental health problem in the nation

What causes anxiety disorders? While researchers have identified certain biological underpinnings, a "cure" has not yet been found. But now, a new book by a noted anxiety specialist (herself a recovered agoraphobic) has helped to put anxiety sufferers on the road to recovery. Her landmark approach finally addresses a comprehensive perspective for a productive solution.

Psychotherapist Lynne Freeman suffered a panic attack some years ago while an undergraduate psychology student. She enlisted the help of a well respected psychologist. The more frequent and intense her panic episodes grew, the more frustrated she and her doctor became. After a year's effort of trying to pinpoint the cause of her disorder, the doctor regretfully terminated treatment.

For Dr. Freeman, the trauma of being dismissed with no hope for improvement left her totally agoraphobic, a shut-in. After several years, she set out to overcome the condition herself. She devised her own treatment methods, and when she had at last progressed far enough to resume her schooling, she eagerly poured over all the latest research data on panic disorder, using what findings were appropriate to accelerate her rehabilitation.

Determined to help others suffering a similar plight, Dr. Freeman went on to obtain an M.A. and then a Ph.D. in Health Administration. Her in-depth doctoral research study on anxiety disorders drew praise from colleagues. Once in private practice, she began to apply the innovative methods used for her own recovery with her patients.

After seven years of success with these techniques, Dr. Freeman established a full-service treatment facility for individuals suffering from both anxiety and depression. The result was *Open Doors Institute*, based in Los Angeles where she serves as Director, employing a panel of psychotherapists trained in her unique methodology.

Dr. Freeman's breakthrough approaches have gained her wide-ranging recognition throughout the mental health community. She lectures extensively and appears frequently on national television and radio programs.

INDEX